BOND INVESTING FOR BE-GINNERS

PROTECTING WEALTH AND GENERATING INCOME EVEN DURING MARKET DOWNTURNS

RILEY WHITMAN

Copyright © 2025 BY SYNAST PUBLISHING

Published by SYNAST PUBLISHING

ISBN: 978-1-968418-20-5

INTRODUCTION

In today's unpredictable financial landscape, investors are increasingly seeking strategies that not only safeguard their wealth but also generate reliable income streams. Bonds have long stood as a cornerstone of such strategies, offering a balance of risk and return that appeals to both novice and experienced investors. However, the world of bond investing is often perceived as complex, shrouded in financial jargon, and intricate dynamics that can intimidate newcomers. This book aims to demystify the intricacies of bond investing, providing a comprehensive guide that empowers readers to make informed decisions, even during market downturns.

Understanding bonds as fundamental financial instruments is crucial; they are essentially loans made by investors to borrowers, typically corporations or governments, with the promise of periodic interest payments and the return of principal at maturity. This book breaks down these concepts into digestible insights, illustrating how bonds can serve as tools for income generation, capital preservation, and diversification. Through historical analyses and real-world examples, readers will discover how bonds have historically performed during economic crises, highlighting their role as a stabilizing force in investment portfolios.

Addressing common fears and misconceptions, the book dispels myths that bonds are outdated or overly complex. Instead, it presents bonds as vital components of a well-rounded investment strategy, particularly in volatile markets. The chapters are designed to build a foundation of knowledge, gradually introducing more advanced strategies such as risk management, portfolio diversification, and the evaluation of specialized bond types like high-yield and municipal bonds.

Readers will find practical guidance on constructing bond portfolios tailored to their specific financial goals and risk profiles. Whether you are new to investing or looking to refine your existing strategy, this book offers actionable insights and tools to navigate the bond market effectively. With a focus on clarity and practicality, it aims to equip you with the confidence and knowledge necessary to protect and grow your wealth through intelligent bond investing.

Table of Contents

INTRODUCTION   3

Table of Contents   v

Chapter 01: Introduction to Bonds   1

    Understanding Bonds   1
    The Role of Bonds in Portfolios   3
    Common Misconceptions   4
    The Economic Importance of Bonds   6

Chapter 02: Bond Types and Structures   9

    Treasuries and Municipals   9
    Corporate and Green Bonds   11
    Understanding Coupon Structures   12
    Maturity Profiles and Embedded Options   14

Chapter 03: Pricing and Yield Calculations   16

    How Bond Prices Are Set   16
    Yield to Maturity and Its Importance   17
    Yield to Call and Yield to Worst   19
    Accrued Interest and Trade Settlements   21

Chapter 04: Market Dynamics and Bond Trading   23

    Primary vs. Secondary Markets   23
    Trading Platforms and Innovations   25
    Liquidity and Price Discovery   27
    Common Trading Mistakes   29

Chapter 05: Risk Management in Bond Investing   31

    Understanding Duration and Convexity   31
    Credit Risk Assessment   33
    Scenario Analysis for Risk Management   35

Hedging Techniques   36

Chapter 06: Portfolio Construction Strategies   39

Building a Bond Ladder   39
Barbell and Bullet Strategies   41
Diversification in Fixed Income   42
Rebalancing Bond Portfolios   44

Chapter 07: Tax Efficiency and Regulations   47

Taxable vs. Tax-Exempt Bonds   47
Calculating After-Tax Yield   49
Navigating Regulatory Changes   50
IRS Rules and Compliance   52

Chapter 08: Advanced Bond Instruments   55

High-Yield Bonds and Due Diligence   55
Mortgage-Backed Securities   57
Inflation-Protected Bonds and FRNs   58
Green Bonds and ESG Considerations   60

Chapter 09: Bond Funds and ETFs   63

ETFs vs. Individual Bonds   63
Mutual Funds and Closed-End Funds   65
Hidden Risks in Pooled Products   67
Evaluating Fund Managers   68

Chapter 10: Tools and Resources for Bond Investors   71

Digital Tools for Bond Analysis   71
Leveraging Peer Communities   73
Ongoing Learning and Education   75
Building a Lifelong Learning System   76

Chapter 11: Market Watch and Adapting Strategies   79

Monitoring Macroeconomic Changes   79
Adjusting Portfolios for Market Shifts   81

Evaluating Product Innovations   83
Proactive Portfolio Review   85

Chapter 12: Execution and Order Placement   87

Placing Orders Online   87
Avoiding Execution Mistakes   89
Understanding Order Types   90
Using Checklists for Success   92

Chapter 13: Real-World Case Studies   95

Market Turmoil and Bond Portfolios   95
Case Studies in Bond Mispricing   97
Successful Bond Investing Strategies   98
Learning from Mistakes   100

Chapter 14: Conclusion and Next Steps   103

Recap of Key Concepts   103
Empowering the Bond Investor   105
Engaging with Community Resources   107
The Path Forward in Bond Investing   109

EPILOGUE   111

Chapter 01: Introduction to Bonds

Understanding Bonds

Bonds play a significant role in the world of finance as they are the instrument of both personal and institutional investors. Bonds are loans between investors and borrowers, who, in general, are corporate or government borrowers. Buying a bond is a way of lending money to an issuer whereby the investor receives periodic interest and repayment of the face value at the end of the period.

A bond has a number of crucial constituents: the principal, the interest, and the maturity date. The value of a bond that is paid out to the bondholder at the end of the stipulated period is referred to as the principal, face value, or par value. Interest, more commonly known as a coupon, is what is paid to the bondholder, usually twice per year, in exchange for their money. The maturity date is the time when the issuer repays the principal of the bond.

The entity bonds are very important in asset allocations and risk management practices. They appreciate receiving stable income and maintaining and stabilizing capital in portfolios, especially in times of market fluctuations. Traditionally, bonds are known to perform better than stocks in a bear market, which acts as a cushion against equity risk. That feature is what makes them an essential part of a well-balanced investment strategy, particularly for those who have reduced portfolio volatility as a priority.

Bonds are not very popular because they are considered to be complicated and archaic. The recent conditions on the market confirm their relevance. As an example, bonds may provide a stabilized income and smooth out uncertainties in the economy or changes in the rates of interest. They provide a wide assortment of structures, including fixed-rate, floating-rate, zero-coupon, and step-up bonds, all of which have different payment conventions and risk profiles.

Fixed-rate bonds are predictable sources of income, whereas floating-rate bonds will adjust their interest payments depending on the benchmark rates, which may act as a guard against rising interest rates. Zero-coupon notes and issues are sold at a steep discount to offer a lump-sum payment upon maturity. They are very interested in those that require long-term capital appreciation. Bonds that increase in interest rate over time, so-called step-up bonds, can serve as an inflation hedge.

Further, bonds have call, put, and convertibility options embedded in them, which affect the yield and risk of the bond. Callable bonds are those that are re-purchased by their issuer prior to maturity, usually in cases where the interest rate has lowered, thus yielding greater returns as a trade-off. The advantage to issuers of putable bonds is that the bonds offer protection against increased rates by giving the investors the right to sell the bond back to the issuer at certain times. Convertible bonds provide an equity-fixed-income combination because they give the bond the flexibility of converting into a certain number of shares.

In the current investment environment, bonds play an important role in the realization of financial goals such as stable income, retirement planning, and risk-adjusted growth. They are usually perceived as a sleep-well-at-night allocation, giving security and a comfortable income to those investors who want to spend less time at night worrying. Being aware of several types of bonds and their characteristics, and knowing how to organize the portfolio depending on personal considerations and market expectations, investors can have bonds as a vital addition to their diversified investment plan.

The Role of Bonds in Portfolios

Bonds play a very different and much more multidimensional role in the complex ecosystem of investment portfolios than the mere concept of fixed income. Such financial instruments form the core of a balanced portfolio and have stability, income, and diversification as benefits. They play a significant role in building portfolios, which are sensitive to market fluctuations, so that they fit the risk attitude of an investor and their financial objectives.

The essence of bonds is an exclusive kind of loan in which the investor serves as a borrower to the recipient, or issuer (a corporation, government, or municipality). The terms of this arrangement are institutionalized in a bond contract, which defines the terms of the loan, such as the amount to be borrowed, the rate of interest to be charged, and the due date. Bond cash flows are predictable, and this offers the investor an opportunity to have a regular stream of income as well as preserve capital.

The counteracting of the more elastic equity portfolio components is one of the main functions of bonds. In the past, bonds have shown the capability of reducing risk on portfolios, particularly in the upturn of the economy. As an example, bonds tend to perform better than stocks in a market crash, like the crashes in 2008 and 2020, and therefore act as a safe harbor and save investor capital. This is an important feature of bonds because it is used to cushion the returns of a portfolio, so that none of the returns of the portfolio move in a rampage or in a heavily fluctuating way.

Also, bonds play a great role in providing income, especially to those investors who focus more on their cash flows rather than capital gains. It will be of particular importance to retirees or individuals who are close to retirement, as they depend on the consistent payment of interest due on bonds to sustain their lifestyles. Bonds are used to provide flexibility in terms of being able to provide an array of product options, such as fixed-rate, floating-rate, and inflation-linked issues, to suit varying income requirements and inflation hedging requirements.

The next element where bonds excel is diversification. A portfolio that includes bonds would enable the investors to have more diversified risk in terms of the asset types, sectors, and geographies. This diversification minimizes the amount of risk in the portfolio as a whole and increases its chances of stable returns. There is also diversification by investor base, including government bonds, corporate bonds, municipal bonds, and emerging market debt, each with different risk-reward qualities.

Moreover, bonds are strategic in asset allocation, which is a very important aspect of portfolio management. Asset allocation is a way to decide the right proportion of asset classes to meet the risk tolerance level of the investor, investment horizon, and other financial needs. Bonds can be very useful in conservative and balanced portfolios, as they have more predictable returns and lower relative risk compared to stocks. They assist in the realization of the desired risk-return profile and also assist in strategic rebalancing of the portfolio over time.

Bonds are very important in the constitution and maintenance of portfolios. They are stable, yield, and diversified; thus, they are good investment decisions, especially with the risk-averse investor or investor intending to merely preserve capital, a habitual flow of income is justified. With the help of the multifunctionality of the bonds, investors can easily handle the vagaries of portfolio management and become more solid in terms of finances in the changing environment of the market.

Common Misconceptions

There are so many myths surrounding the practice of bond investing, which usually impedes the decision-making process of both new and experienced investors. Such errors in perceptions may distort the perceptions of investment risk and returns, which could result in inappropriate investment decisions. One of the most common features is a belief that bonds are safe investments (the idea that bonds are always safe). Although bonds have always been associated with stability in comparison with stocks, there are associated risks of interest rate risk, credit risk, and inflation risk. An interest rate risk, for example, may cause a price fluctuation in the case of long-term bonds because rates fluctuate. An increasing interest rate may lead to a decrease in the value of bonds, a factor that may destroy the value of the principal of an investment.

The other fallacy is that bonds are dull or not as lucrative in returns as the other areas of assets. This perception does not account for much of the strategic considerations that bonds may offer a diversified portfolio. Bonds may serve as an income stream with the interest payments and help smooth out returns in times when there is a high level of fluctuation in the equity market. In addition, some bond tactics, including investing in high-yield bonds or applying bond ladders, are effective at getting competitive returns on the one hand, and controlling risk on the other hand.

Another myth that should be refuted is the misconception about bonds as an instrument that conservative, risk-averse investors can use. Although bonds are definitely an attractive asset to stability fee-seekers, they are also desired by investment-seekers. When the equity market is performing dismally, the bond can be used to hedge, give liquidity, and hold the possibility of appreciating the capital in some market situations. As an example, when the interest rate starts dropping, then the bonds already owned may increase in value and thus provide capital gains to the investor.

Another major misconception regarding bond markets exists, which is the assumption of complexity. It is not a secret that a lot of people consider the bond market to be too complicated, full of mysterious language and structures that are challenging to navigate. As much as it is a fact that there is some complexity to bond markets, there can be a simplification of the process, and a grasping of the fundamentals to enable an investor to be armed with these facts and make more informed decisions. There are tools and resources to make the concepts simpler and the process of bond investing open to all.

The other mistake is the assumption that economic changes have the same effect on all bonds. As it stands, not all kinds of bonds are the same in terms of responding to changes caused by economic dynamics. As an illustration, inflation-adjusted bonds (TIPS) increase in price with inflation. Thus, it may be desirable to use such securities in an inflationary setting, whereas in high-tax situations, municipal (tax-free) bonds may provide tax benefits.

Lastly, certain investors may erroneously believe that the role of bonds becomes insignificant in the era of low-interest rates. Nevertheless, bonds cannot be disregarded when it comes to portfolio diversification and risk management. Bonds tend to lower the total volatility of a portfolio, and they are a source of certain income. Moreover, the choice of bonds, including the one based on concentration on the credit quality of securities or the search of bond markets abroad, might reveal opportunities notwithstanding the low-rate environment.

It is important to overcome these myths to ensure that bond investing is fully utilized. With the awareness of the reality of bonds and their place in a diversified investment portfolio, the investor is more capable of constructing the proposition the bond market offers, and, finally, improving their financial performance.

The Economic Importance of Bonds

Bonds are an essential element of the contemporary economic system that would be weakened to a fatal degree without these instruments. Their meaning goes further than that of a mere investment vehicle; they are pillars that form the basis of financial stability and economic progress. Bonds are simply debts, and they are issued through governments, municipalities, or corporations to facilitate the raising of capital. Such capital is usually channelled into infrastructure programmes, expansion activities, or other such heavy spending ventures that feed into economic growth.

The contribution of bonds in the stabilization of economies cannot be overestimated. In times when the economy is uncertain or even in recession periods, bonds are a better alternative investment option to the equity market, which can be very dynamic. They guarantee certain cash flow in terms of regular fixed interest-related payments, called coupons, and are more suitable for investors who want less risk. This predictability is more appealing, especially in instances where the stock markets are affected by increased volatility, like in the case of financial crises.

Besides, bonds are instrumental when it comes to the implementation of monetary policy. The government bonds are a principal mechanism that is used by central banks all over the globe to control the activity of the economy. This is because by purchasing or selling these securities, the central banks can manipulate interest rates and the supply of money. An example of this is when an economy is experiencing a slowdown; the central banks can buy government bonds as a way of injecting liquidity into the economy by lowering interest rates, which would promote borrowing and investment.

Another aspect of the economic relevance of bonds is the diversification advantage that they bring to the table. Bonds can be used to diversify a portfolio in a way that balances out the risks of equities. This is attributed to the fact that bonds mostly have a negative/low correlation to stocks, which means that if stocks underperform, then bonds have the upper hand of doing well. This feature renders risk management strategies, having them as part of it, which will enable the investor to have a more consistent return profile.

Corporate bonds, especially, are crucial in the development and innovation of businesses. Through them, companies can find ways of raising funds without necessarily diluting control through equity issuance. This would allow the businesses to expand, diversify into new markets, or venture into research and development that develops the economy and provides job generation. Also, the interest on corporate bonds is tax-deductible, which is a plus in terms of the bottom line of a company.

Macroeconomically, bonds have an effect on the economic situation as a whole, with the use of the yield curve that demonstrates how the interest rates and the maturity of a debt are interrelated. The yield curve is coded in a manner that the shape of the yield curve can be used to signal investors' preconceptions of the state of the economy, including expectations of growth and inflation. An increase in the steepening of the yield curve, in this example, may imply a future rise in the economy, whereas an inverted one would signal that a recession is about to happen.

In addition, bonds are used to finance state projects that improve the welfare of society. Munis are used to fund community infrastructure in roads, schools, and hospitals, and increase the economic and social well-being of the community. These projects not only enhance the quality of life but also help local economies thrive as they provide employment and business activities.

To summarize, it can be stated that bonds are not mere financial tools; they are also the wheels in the machine of the economy. The fact that they ensure a stable environment, economic expansion, and safeguard the welfare of the people is a testament to their absolute necessity in the economies of any nation and international areas. Therefore, learning about the economic significance of bonds is of immense importance to investors, policymakers, and any individual keen on how the financial system operates.

Chapter 02: Bond Types and Structures

Treasuries and Municipals

U.S. Treasuries are part of the bedrock of the world of fixed-income investments. Treasuries are bonds published by the U.S. Department of the Treasury, and hence they are almost risk-free because the full faith and credit of the U.S. government supports them. They are a reference point in the bond market, which is used to set up the prices of a plethora of other financial instruments. They are usually viewed as a haven by the investors, especially when there is market volatility or economic uncertainty. Treasuries can be obtained in many forms, such as Treasury Bills (T-Bills), Treasury Notes, and Treasury Bonds, which are differentiated in terms of their maturity and interest payment schemes. The T-Bills are short-term securities that can run up to a year or less, whereas the Treasury Notes and bonds are longer-term securities, and they have a maturity rate of two to thirty years.

Treasuries' pricing and liquidity depend on some variables such as changes in interest rates, inflationary expectations, and macroeconomic policies. The 10-year investors especially monitor Treasury Notes as an instrument in determining the interest rates and economic well-being. The interest rate is a benchmark of mortgage rates and corporate bond spreads, which affect the costs of all loans in the economy. Treasuries are traded in the secondary market quite liberally and have high liquidity, thus enabling an investor to buy and sell them relatively easily.

Municipal bonds, or munis, have another set of characteristics and factors to be considered. State and local governments issue these bonds to finance town-wide projects, e.g., roads, highways, and schools, among others. The major asset of the municipal bonds is their tax-exemption status, which, in many cases, includes the interest increase both at the federal and, when the investor lives in the given state, at the state and local levels. This tax advantage has the potential to bring about favorable after-tax returns, making the munis very attractive to investors in higher tax brackets.

Nevertheless, municipal bond assessment involves a complex awareness of the tax-related aspects involving the credit risks of the municipal bonds. Heightened muni yields: Since munis do not carry with them the definite guarantee of the federal government, their credit quality is determined by the financial state of the issuing municipality. The risks posed by credit ratings of bond evaluation agencies such as Moody's or Standard and Poor would be a good indicator of this risk. Still, a careful evaluation of the local economy and the source of revenues that have exactly backed these bonds will also have to be present.

Municipal bonds are divided into general obligation bonds and revenue bonds, confined by either the taxation authority of the issuer or by a particular source of income of the issue, such as toll roads or utility plants. Since municipals can be tax-exempt, the issue may be complicated because some bonds are covered under the Alternative Minimum Tax (AMT), making them inappropriate to some investors.

Overall, treasuries and municipal bonds are crucial components of the fixed income portfolio and have their unique advantages and factors. Treasuries are unmatched sources of security and liquidity and are the benchmark in the world bond market. Conversely, municipal bonds can present tax benefits and the opportunity to invest in local ventures; however, this investing will need to have credit and taxes considered. The pair offers investors a wide range of income-generating opportunities, diversification, and risk mitigation.

Corporate and Green Bonds

Corporate bonds form an important type of bond investment in which investors are presented with an opportunity to get involved in the financial well-being as well as the development of corporations. The bonds are basically a type of debt securities sold by companies to obtain capital to undertake different purposes, including expansion, running an operation, or refinancing an existing debt. Corporate bonds will be attractive as there is a possibility of higher yields than government securities because corporate credit profiles are higher risk in nature. There are credit ratings that investors have to walk through, which are used to evaluate the issuer's ability to pay. The agencies, such as Moody's, Standard & Poor's, and Fitch, have been giving these ratings, which act as a road map in determining the risk involved in the process.

Bonds issued by companies come in a variety of varieties, covering different sectors and credit ratings, as well as high-grade investing opportunities and high-yield or junk bonds. The latter has a bigger return with more risk; thus, they fare best with individuals who have high risk tolerance. On the other hand, investment-grade bonds are issued by well-rated companies and are thus less risky but tend to offer lower returns in general. Investors must understand the complexities of corporate bond covenants, which are attached to the bond and make up the terms and conditions of the bond. These covenants cushion the investors by putting limits on any moves by the companies that may incur the inability of the companies to repay their debt.

On another parallel, there has been the rise of the green bond within the burgeoning ecosystem of sustainable finance. These bonds will specifically be designed to finance projects that can offer a positive influence on the environment in the form of renewable energy, energy efficiency, or clean transportation. Green bond demand is fuelled by the growing importance of the environment, social, and governance (ESG) criteria with respect to investment decisions. Green bonds are a two-purpose instrument used by issuers because not only do they help to raise capital, but they can also boost the environmental credibility and attract those investors who are socially responsible.

The supply side, the actual market of green bonds, is facilitated through the Green Bond Principles, which give guidance on the proceeds usage, project quality, and disclosures to be transparent and accountable. Green bond investors are usually willing to invest not only to obtain financial gains but also to feel that they have participated in or contributed to the sustainability of the environment. The actual positive impact of the green bonds may, however, be difficult to ascertain since it involves rigorous testing of the sustainability and devotion of the issuer and the outcomes of the environmental health of the projects funded.

Corporate and green bonds are important parts of a diversified bond portfolio. Corporate bonds provide a combination of risk and yield, as well as different amounts of credit risk and yield possibilities. Green bonds are also sold at a reduced rate of interest as compared to conventional corporate bonds, as the investments are transacted in accordance with individual or institutional values of sustainability and social responsibility. With the changing nature of the marketplace of such bonds, investors are already being urged to weigh up measures of finance, as well as an overall impact on ESG, by including such measurements in portfolio selection with the aim of not only expecting a profitable outcome but also a positive contribution to our world.

Understanding Coupon Structures

When analysing the landscape of bond investments, the coupon structure of the bond plays a central role that an investor must understand before making a decision. Coupons are more or less the interest that is paid on bonds, and the structure of the coupon can have a lot of impact on the yield and the risk associated with the bond. There are differences in structure and features of the various types of coupons, as well as important differences between them in terms of implications to investors.

Fixed-rate bonds are some of the simplest, in that the bond issues a fixed payment of interest over its lifetime. It makes them attractive to conservative investors who are interested in a stable income. They are also not flexible in changing interest rate periods, and there is the danger of an opportunity cost of rising interest rates.

On the other hand, floating-rate bonds change their coupon payments in relation to some other interest rate index, often the LIBOR or the federal funds rate. The bonds are offering protection against increasing rates since their payments will rise with the index. They, however, bring about uncertainty in the future income flow, which is inappropriate for those who are in need of stable cash flows.

Zero-coupon bonds, in turn, do not provide periodical interest. Rather, they are sold at a discount of their face value and repay the face value at maturity. This structure is advantageous to investors who do not depend on the present income but on the future gains. Failure to make an income up to a certain amount periodically follows, which is beneficial to tax-deferred accounts since the investor does not confront the realization of an income until maturity.

Step-up bonds take a middle ground by allowing the rate of the coupon to change at designated rates of time over the lifetime of the bond. Such a structure may be appealing in a higher interest rate environment, where one can get a rising income and limited predictability. The initial yield can, however, be less than that of the fixed-rate bonds, and this brings in the need to make a judgment on future rate expectations.

The consideration of the different forms of coupons is essential in this alignment of bond investments to personal financial targets and market conditions. All the structures offer both benefits and drawbacks and have implications on the risk and reward of the investment. Investors have to balance such factors by ensuring that they meet their income requirements, interest rate prospects, and their risk tolerance when choosing suitable bonds to include in their portfolio. By so doing, they can be in a position to handle their investments appropriately so that they can realize the desired financial results.

Maturity Profiles and Embedded Options

Maturity profiles and embedded options are essential in the bond investment world, in that they are important factors in the creation of a well-established portfolio. Maturity profiles that cover how bond payments are to be made determine the sensitivity of a bond towards changes in interest rate; hence, the maturity profile is quite critical to the investor's strategy. Generally, bonds are classified into short-term, intermediate, and long-term maturities, which have separate qualities and impacts on investors' portfolios.

Arguments in favour of short-term bonds, usually with a maturity period of less than five years, are the reduced interest rate sensitivity and a steady, predictable source of income. They are especially attractive when interest rates are rising, and reinvestment opportunities offer attractive interest rates. In contrast, long-term bonds, which may be longer than ten years, are more prone to fluctuations in rate, yielding high returns at higher volatility levels. Such bonds may perform well during a deflationary environment, an aspect of them to hedge against economic crashes because they yield a fixed income.

Intermediate-term bonds hold a middle ground and provide average responsiveness to rate fluctuations and a combination of lower income potential and growth. Much of the time, investors utilize these bonds to fill the liquidity gap between short-term investments and the lucrative long-term choices. The tactical choice of maturity in bonds enables the investor to optimize his or her portfolio to fit the financial objectives, risk tolerance, and market projections.

Additional complexity, as well as the possibility of bond investing, can be found in the embedded options. Such characteristics as callable, putable, or convertible options can have a great influence on the risk and returns of a bond. Callable bonds allow the issuer to redeem the bond before it is due, thereby giving them the choice to do so at a premium. This is beneficial to the issuers who thrive in the declining interest rate because they can refinance at better rates. However, as far as investors are concerned, callable bonds can give rise to reinvestment risk since they may be forced to reinvest at a low market rate if the bond is called prematurely.

The puttable bond, however, gives its investors the option to sell the bond back to the issuer at fixed dates prior to maturity. This aspect is of substantial benefit during the high-interest-rate environment, which also gives protection against negative prices in the bonds. Convertible bonds provide an unusual combination of fixed-income and equity investments because these bonds can be transformed into a certain number of stocks issued by the company in which the bonds are issued. It is an opportunity to maximize returns in bull markets of equities and a good means to diversify and expand.

These embedded options are critical in the knowledge required by the investors who would wish to take calculated risks to achieve their goals. By analyzing the implications of these features, investors will be able to design their strategies in a manner that yields the best results and in a way that risks are well managed. A coherent investment strategy combining maturity profiles and embedded options enables the investor in the bond market to operate in the fine detail provided by the bond market universe and reach a composition that satisfies the requirement to balance the portfolio and remain faithful to the investor's goal.

Chapter 03: Pricing and Yield Calculations

How Bond Prices Are Set

Bond pricing is an active relationship amongst various forces in the market, and the basic laws of supply and demand prevail. The centerpiece of this mechanism is the interest rates, and this is the main guiding element that determines the valuation of the bonds. The decrease in interest leads to lower yields of existing bonds, and that is why when interest rates increase, existing bonds lose their attractiveness and, thus, lose their market prices. On the other hand, lowering the rates increases the price of the existing bonds that bear higher fixed rates.

Sentiment is essential on the part of investors, too. The actors in the market constantly review the economics of the time, the inflation expectations, and geopolitical incidents, all of which determine the confidence they have in terms of the future stability of their economic environment. To the extent that the riskier bonds are purchased, any positive attitude in the market may increase the price. In contrast, any uncertainty or negative attitude may result in demand shifting to safer, government-backed securities, and this may have an impact on the price levels.

The other key determinant of the bond price is the central bank policies. The bond markets can respond to dramatic changes when central banks announce interest rate adjustments or quantitative easing policy. To illustrate, when a central bank chooses to reduce interest rates, the price of bonds may increase as bond yields all over the market normalize to the new interest rate conditions.

The yields of various bonds differ, and the difference between the yields of various bonds is called spreads and is important in the relative values in the bond market. The creditworthiness of an issuer, represented by credit spreads as well as liquidity represented by liquidity spread, affects the pricing of a bond. A widening spread tends to be a sign of a higher perceived risk or lesser liquidity, and as such, price adjustments would occur.

Investors require the exploitation of a benchmark to determine the value of bonds. Investors commonly use benchmark interest rates to determine whether a particular bond is attractively priced. The 10-year Treasury yield and the London Interbank Offered Rate (LIBOR) are some examples. An example may be that a corporate bond was quoted at a spread over the 10-year Treasury, and this is a good indication of the risk premium that investors required over a risk-free rate.

Bond pricing is not stable in volatile or illiquid markets. In times of stress in the market, e.g., a financial crisis, investors can start congregating on safe assets, and as a result, the spreads on riskier bonds can widen and their prices decline. Astute investors could use this anomaly by trading in environments where mispricings are recognized.

In a real sense, a multi-faceted assortment of economic indicators, market sentiment, and policies influences bond prices. Knowing these factors is important when investors are looking to understand the bond market and make the right investment decisions.

Yield to Maturity and Its Importance

One of the concepts that is of great significance to investors of bonds is the Yield to Maturity (YTM), which represents the entire expected profit on a bond that may be generated over time in case it is held up to the maturity date. It is a complete calculation that adjudicates the current market price of the bond, the coupon interest it will pay, and the face value when the bond matures. It is an important indicator to investors since they will have a uniform gauge for evaluating potential returns of various bonds irrespective of their coupon rates and maturities.

YTM calculation is not a trivial process and may involve iteration or financial calculators. It is obtained by weighing future cash outflows generated by a bond at the present value to its current price in the market. They have periodic coupons on the cash flows and payment of the face value of the bond on maturity. To an investor, it is difficult to manage without comprehending YTM and computing it, as it is the expected rate of yearly income, taking into consideration all elements of the bond's income.

The use of YTM is especially important because it is used as a barometer in making informed investments. It enables the investors to determine the attractiveness of a bond in comparison to the same issue and that of the market. Investors can use YTM to compare returns available in various bonds so as to determine which have better returns on the money they invest, depending on their riskiness. As an example, the bond with a better YTM may appear to be more suitable; however, this may also mean that the bond has higher risk, such as a greater risk of default or fluctuations within the market.

Also, YTM helps in the realization of how the change of interest rates in the market will affect the prices of bonds. Having an increase in interest rates will make the bonds that previously existed, with lower yields, unattractive, which makes them stick in the marketplace, pushing their prices down and thus presenting them with greater yield-to-maturity. On the other hand, during a decline in interest rates, the market value of existing bonds with higher yields increases, and these bonds increase their value, thus decreasing YTM. This is the basic principle of interest rate movement as it relates to fixing interest rates and their impact on bond prices.

Nevertheless, inasmuch as YTM is a potent instrument, it cannot be without constraints. The most frequently used assumption is that a 100 percent reinvestment of the coupons is made at the same rate as the YTM, which is not always practical in changing rate situations. Also, YTM fails to consider the implication of the credit risk of the bond issuer or the risk of early redemption of a callable bond.

Investors should also know the differences between yield measures (YTM) and other values, including current yield and yield to call. Where current yield takes into consideration only the annual amount of payment (coupon) of the bond in relation to the price received in the market, yield to call takes into consideration the fee charged for the bond being called before its maturity. All these measures can give distinct answers, but YTM gives the most detailed answer in long-term investment analysis.

Overall, Yield to Maturity is a metric that investors of bonds cannot ignore; it provides a rich insight into what could be expected in returns, and it also shows the impacts due to the market conditions and the risk considerations. Investors are also in a better position to make better decisions in terms of optimizing their portfolios, both in terms of income and preserving capital, due to the mastery of YTM.

Yield to Call and Yield to Worst

In bond investments, it is vital to appreciate the difference between yields so as to make sound decisions. Some of them are Yield to Call (YTC) and Yield to Worst (YTW), which are critical measures when dealing with bonds containing call options. Yield to Call is the yield of a note or any bond in the event that one were to acquire and hold the bond till the call date. This measure is especially applicable to callable bonds, which are accompanied by a risk that the issuer might decide to repay the bond earlier than its maturing date, particularly when interest rates fall.

In the case of callable bonds, the issuer reserves the option to buy out the bond before its maturity date, usually at a premium. This aspect benefits the issuers in the case of falling interest rate structures because they are able to pay off their debts at a reduced price. To the investors, however, it brings on the element of risk and uncertainty, where the bond can be called away as soon as it becomes more beneficial to invest in it. The yield to call is the calculation that is based on the call price of the bond, the amount of time until that call arrives, and the upcoming coupon payments, which will be paid between the current date and the call date. This yield will give the investors a sense of what they can expect to receive in the event that the bond is called off before its time.

Yield to Worst, on the other hand, is a more conservative yardstick that indicates the lowest value that can be attained on a bond without the face of actual defaulting on the part of the issuer. This indicator considers any call dates and maturity dates and displays the pessimistic projection of yield to investors. Yield to Worst is essential to risk-averse investors because it gives a clear view of the minimum yield they may get (in view that the bond may be called off at any time).

The calculation of YTW is how the yield of possible call dates and maturity date is calculated, as well as the lowest of these calculated yields. The yield is especially useful when the interest rates are volatile, as a bond that is called has more chances in this situation. With the worst-case yield, investors will be in a better position to evaluate the risks that their bond investments could bring them.

Yield concepts are among the most important things to know when making strategic decisions, whether you are a portfolio manager or an individual investor. To some extent, callable bonds may be issued at higher initial yields in order to counter the call-risk factor, and it is the responsibility of the investor to balance this risk with the possible loss of returns in case the bond is called. Comparing Yield to Call and Yield to Worst enables investors to take bonds that are consistent with their level of risk and investment purposes.

Further, the scenario analysis illustrated by these calculations explains why scenario analysis is vital in bond investing. The combination of the best and worst possible outcomes will also allow investors to create portfolios that hold up well to a variety of interest rate climates, as well as the actions taken by the issuers. It is proactive, which eliminates surprises and makes sure that the investment strategy is tied to the rest of the financial objectives.

Briefly, both Yield to Call and Yield to Worst are irreparable in terms of managing the intricacies of callable bonds. They offer invaluable information that enables investors to make decisions that are best suited to their financial goals and risk tastes, like the potential returns and the risks that are involved with these securities. A more systematic understanding of these yield concepts will allow investors to improve their knowledge of bond investing and hence have a more predictable result in their fixed-income investments.

Accrued Interest and Trade Settlements

When we are learning the concepts of investing in bonds, it is imperative to comprehend the details of accrued interest as well as trade settlements, whether one is a first-time or seasoned investor. Accrued interest is the amount of interest accumulated on a bond since the bond was last paid in the form of a coupon. The consideration is of particular significance between coupon redemption dates. The seller of the bond is entitled to the accrued interest to the date of sale of the bond, and the buyer thereafter assumes the responsibility to bear the interest of the bond starting on the date of purchase.

To determine the accrued interest, one has to apply day count conventions, which are standard conventions that help in counting the number of days between two dates. There are different conventions, such as actual/actual, 30/360, and actual/360 methods. All these ways of computing the number of days and interest received are different, thus affecting the amount of money one can receive in settling a bond. For example, a bond that pays semiannual coupons can apply a 30/360 structure, where each month is deemed to have 30 days and a year is composed of 360 days.

Trade settlements, however, are those that refer to the transfer between the buyer and seller of the delivery of the bond and the money. It normally happens within several days of business, based on the trade date. The process of the settlement guarantees that the seller and the buyer will have received both the bond and the money due, along with the interest gained by the owner. By appreciating the specifics of this process, the investors may treat potential shocks and the lack of understanding that a miscalculated amount of money that one owes and the time when the cash flow is to be submitted may cause.

A mistake that very often occurs when taking care of accrued interest is duplication. This arises when investors do not remember to take out the accrued interest when calculating the price of the bond, which will overestimate the yield or the return of the bond. The second common error is that it is often forgotten to count the accrued interest in the total returns, which might mislead an investor about their view on the performance of their investments.

Tables and checklists are useful for helping investors look up information. These are resources that will help to prevent errors at the time of trade or when the portfolio is being reviewed to be sure that the interest generated and the setups are done accurately and recorded. Further, to facilitate valuation, one can use technological aids; however, one should be precise when calculating the price of the bond and the yield on the bond by using Excel or online calculators.

As applied, setting the price of a purchase in a secondary bond market would be the addition of accrued interest to the buying price of a bond. As an example, an investor who purchases a bond at a point between coupon dates will be required to pay the bond's purchaser the price of the bond plus interest that has accrued since the last coupon date. This will guarantee the money back to the seller as a payback of the time he/she had the bond.

By gaining an understanding of these concepts, investors are in a position to approach the bond market with more clarity, hence making decisions that are based on their financial goals. Knowledge of accrued interest and trade settlements not only improves the capability of the investor to manage the portfolio, but also gives them/the knowledge to undertake such strategic trading activities in order to get the maximum and take minimum risks.

Chapter 04: Market Dynamics and Bond Trading

Primary vs. Secondary Markets

The bond investing scenario is highly dependent on two vital stages in the markets, which include the primary and the secondary markets. These markets are the foundation of the bond distribution and the trading of securities. There is an existing relation between them as each market has its significance in the life of security, the first is when it is issued, and the second is when it is traded. It is also critical for any investor who seeks to effectively navigate the bond market to understand these markets in terms of their nuance.

The main market refers to the market where the bonds are first printed. The second phase can be likened to a debutante event of the financial instrument, a sign to indicate that the bonds are being presented to investors in the market. In this market, entities known as issuers (either governments, municipalities, or corporations) sell fresh bonds directly to investors. The primary market plays a pivotal role in providing capital to organisations that need to carry out various activities, finance infrastructure projects, expand their businesses, or even refinance their previous loans. In this stage, the provisions of the bond are established and determined, such as the bond coupon rate, the date on which the principal is to be paid, and the principal amount.

The terms and conditions set forth to investors in the primary market usually apply to a new issue of bonds because they may be auctioned to investors or may also be underwritten by an underwriting syndicate. As an example, government bonds may be auctioned where the bidders with the highest offers are entitled to get the bonds. Investment banks usually sell corporate bonds; on the other hand, investment banks underwrite the issuance of bonds by purchasing the entire issue and reselling it to the investors. This is done so that the issuer has the money needed immediately, and the investment bank assumes the risk of selling the bonds in the market.

After the bonds have been issued into the primary market, they transfer to the secondary market. In this case, bonds are sold among the investors just like the buying and selling of stocks in the stock market. There is liquidity via the secondary market, which enables buyers and sellers to trade in the bonds prior to maturity. Such a market is crucial to continuing a positive image of bonds as an investment class. It is where price discovery occurs and allows investors to react to the movement of the market.

On the secondary market, the price of a bond may vary, depending on many different factors, including changes in interest rates, the credit quality of the issuer, and the well-being of the economy. An example is that when interest rates increase, any of the previously issued bonds with lower interest rates will not be favorably regarded, and as such, the price of such bonds will drop. A drop in interest rates, on the other hand, can and will make previous bonds more attractive, and it will increase the price of the associated bond. This is the flexibility of the secondary market, which enables investors to take advantage of the market trends that can result in gains by selling off the bonds at a higher rate compared to the prices at which they were bought.

Bid-ask spread also characterizes the secondary market, and it is the difference between the price that sellers are willing to sell their stocks (ask price) and the price that buyers are ready to pay the sellers (bid price). The tighter the spread, the more liquid the market and the easier it will be, as an investor, to conduct a trade without making a large price concession.

The technological innovations have also revolutionized the secondary market with online platforms that make the market more transparent and accessible. These are electronic websites where investors can exchange and trade bonds more effectively, at the same time providing them with real-time data and analytical information.

To sum up, both the primary and secondary markets are interconnected with the functioning of the bond market ecosystem. Whilst the primary market allows funds to be raised by means of new bond issues, the secondary market allows the investor the flexibility and liquidity required. Combined, they create a strong system on which bond investing is based, which serves to meet the needs of both issuers and investors.

Trading Platforms and Innovations

In the context of bond investment, innovation and changes brought about by the upgrading of the trading platforms have greatly changed the manner in which investors relate to the market. The introduction of digital components has democratized bond markets, making them accessible to individual investors rather than allowing them to be the preserve of institutional players. The emergence of this shift can be described by the greater level of transparency, accessibility, and efficiency in the bond trading environment.

Online trading has made the process of buying bonds much easier since the investor can easily maneuver through the various alternatives available. These platforms have easy-to-use interfaces that guide investors in choosing bonds depending on respective parameters like maturity, yield, and credit rating. The bonds are easily accessible, and this has widened the investor base, giving more people access to the bonds without necessarily having to have deep knowledge about finance.

Advanced analytics and research tools have also become a part of trading platforms, becoming one of the crucial innovations in the sphere. A credible risk analysis of bond issues has now been made available to investors, who can compare historical ratings and performance of a bond issue and its risk parameters. The abundance of information enables investors to make educated decisions to create a tailor-made portfolio in terms of investment goals and appetite.

In addition, real-time data feeds and alerts have been included in trading platforms, so that when investors are trading, they are updated with the changes that occurred, such as market flows and news, which may cause fluctuations in bond prices. The instant availability of information is worth considering, especially when taking investment decisions, especially in uncertain market conditions when prices of bonds may change at a dizzying speed.

Improved liquidity in the markets is a factor that the increase in the use of electronic trading has met. Electronic trading systems enable a more effective matching of buyers and sellers, avoiding the cost and time expenditure in making the trade. The increased liquidity is especially useful in the bond market, where historically, some issues of bonds may have been hard to buy or sell in a short period since the trade volume was low.

Also, the creation of digital bond platforms has started using such innovative products as smart beta and factor-based ETFs that help investors gain exposure to customized bond portfolios that match specific investment strategies. These products allow investors to gain exposure to diversified bond portfolios without the need to make their coupon-by-coupon choices and manage each of these bonds individually, conveniently, and at a low cost.

Online networks have also given rise to peer communities of social investing and peer networks where investors have access to a pool of information, investing insights, and strategies. These communities form a good source of learning and interacting, and add good value to the investing experience by giving them access to collective wisdom and crowd-sourced information.

Besides these developments, the sustainability and ethical investing trend has given rise to platforms that provide ESG (Environmental, Social, and Governance) bond-investing opportunities. These portals offer such tools as the assessment of impact and sustainability of bond issuers, portfolio alignment with values, and social missions.

Constant change in the trading platforms and new products in the financial field is revolutionizing the bond investment market. Advances in technology are bound to result in even more organizational efficiency and ability, transparency, and personalization of bond trading activities, which is an indicator that bond investing will become increasingly approachable and in line with the current investment processes and goals.

Liquidity and Price Discovery

In complex bond investing, both liquidity and price discovery are vital in shaping the market itself, and they have significant implications for investor actions. These notions are important in initiating the novice into the world of bond trading and investing in issues of complexity.

Liquidity, as used in the bond markets, refers to an element of ease whereby a bond can be sold or purchased in the bond market with no major effect on its price. Liquidity is linked to the high turnover of funds of a market to enable transactions to take place in a fast and efficient manner, and they often work at the prices immediately before the last trade price. Conversely, low levels of liquidity may bring about a high occurrence of undesirable fluctuations in the names of the commodity, as there are low levels of buyers and sellers who will make the sales possible. This may be a big challenge to investors who are in niche markets or investors who have less turnover.

In the secondary bond market, where trading in bonds takes place after the bonds are originally sold, it is noted that different types of bonds have varying degrees of liquidity. The liquidity of U.S. Treasuries or government bonds in general is high because they are very common and sought after. Corporate bonds, and particularly smaller or less creditworthy corporate ones, may, on the other hand, be less liquid. The impact of this inequality is that the investor can get in and out of a position with more or less speed and expense.

The price discovery refers to the process through which the buyers and sellers in the market set the price of a bond as a result of the interaction. It is part of the market that plays a crucial role, which incorporates the general determination of a bond's value using the available information. Examples of factors that influence price discovery are interest rates, credit ratings, economic indicators, and market participants' perceptions of them. Liquidity and efficiency of price discovery are often measured by the difference between what a buyer is prepared to pay (bid) and what a seller is prepared to accept (ask), i.e., the bid-ask spread. A narrow spread can be indicative of an efficient predictive market, which has good price discovery, and, on the contrary, a wide spread can be indicative of an inefficient predictive market.

The liquidity and price discovery play a role in investment strategy and risk management in practical terms. When an investor does its due diligence work on bonds, it ought to consider the bond liquidity, so that it knows that another bond that holds the same cashflows may have a higher market liquidity, that it will need less time to sell, or it may have to accept a higher price concession to sell. Moreover, price discovery may assist an investor in making a relevant decision on whether to sell or buy a stock based on how the process works.

The introduction of technology and the regulation of markets have also affected the markets in terms of liquidity and price discovery of bonds. Investor access to the prices is improved and costs are lowered due to the promotion of transparency and accessibility of electronic trading platforms, which enables investors to see prices and execute trades in real-time. Also, regulatory efforts to enhance market transparency have helped in the realization of more precise price discovery in favor of both individual and institutional shareholders.

Finally, a clear understanding of the notions of liquidity and price discovery will provide wet-fingered investors with the skills to operate better in the bond market. Through these ideas, investors are able to have better control over their portfolios and trading strategies and reduce any risk related to illiquid markets, inefficient price discovery, etc. Now that beginners start exploring bond investment, being sensitive to the dynamics of liquidity and the dynamics of price discovery can go a long way in enabling them to meet their financial goals.

Common Trading Mistakes

The promise of potential returns in the bond investing world tends to look the other way at the investors and leaves them exposed to the dangers that await them. Errors in trading bonds may prove to be quite expensive, but most of the time, they can go unnoticed with proper knowledge of the situation. A common one is overpayment in thin markets. Occasionally, investors make the mistake of allowing a big spread, and they end up paying more than they are supposed to because they are in a hurry or do not understand the market. This error is especially pronounced in the case of trading corporate bonds, where illiquidity may abound, and spreads may blow out at any time.

The other common mistake is the buying of bonds that are traded only sparingly or even completely non-traded, which is sometimes termed as dead CUSIPs. Such bonds may be little-traded or dated, and investors may find these bonds in illiquid positions; they can end up paying heavily to roll out of them. This tends to be made worse when the investors do not take into account the liquidity profile of a bond being purchased, just based on the yield and not on the market depth.

A similar lack of knowledge concerning the taxes on municipal bonds causes mistakes quite often. This is the implication of acquiring a bond without taking into consideration the non-taxable status of the bond, which can easily change the anticipated yield spectacularly. The same case applies when purchasing foreign bonds without noting the currency settlement risks, because it may expose the buyer to such financial risks unexpectedly. The discussed scenarios contribute to making due diligence and familiarity with the peculiarities of different types of bonds significant.

Trading mistakes are also coupled with execution mistakes. These are the wrong types of orders and a failure to agree on the settlement terms. The thin markets provide investors with the possibility of placing a market order in markets where a sudden change is demanded and sudden price spikes are created. Alternatively, the absence of verification of interest accrual or time of settlement may result in discrepancies between the anticipated and actual returns.

A good checklist can be of great use to overcome these problems. Price, yield, liquidity, and settlement are some of the factors that can be checked before engaging in any trade, thereby evading any of their traps. When speaking of mistakes, investors are advised to notice that the most helpful thing one can do with them is to learn from the mistakes that others made and remain patient and constantly educate oneself, as the key to successful trading.

In addition, it is important to know the dynamics of various trading environments. Municipal, corporate, and international bonds are three different aspects, each of which is a challenge that requires its own strategies. As an example, municipal bonds usually come with certain tax implications, whereas international bonds can create certain currency risks that have to be addressed.

Investors ought to have an active bond trading style, thus utilizing case studies and examples in the real world to appreciate and avoid basic mistakes. In the process, they would be able to develop a factorial trading experience that would be disciplined and minimize risk, as well as maximize returns. Due diligence is crucial, and it is the foundation of a prosperous bond trading.

In one sense, to prevent the pitfalls of trading in bond investing, one will need a combination of knowledge, game planning, and attention. Being aware of the indications of potential traps, as well as having adequate tools and attitude, investors can better enjoy and succeed in the bond markets.

Chapter 05: Risk Management in Bond Investing

Understanding Duration and Convexity

When it comes to investing in bonds, duration and convexity come into play in handling issues considered as interest rate risks and maximizing the performance of investing. Duration is a critical term that determines how interest rates on a bond are affected by the change in the rate of interest, indicating the price change in the bond that will flow as a result of the change in the rate of interest. It is basically a weighted average of the time to capture the cash streams of the bond, and this is in years. Duration measures the sensitivity of a bond price to a change in interest rates by estimating the percentage change in the price of a bond given a 1 percent change in interest rates.

Duration will take different forms, and the most common ones are Macaulay duration and modified duration. Macaulay duration gives the average time it takes to receive all the cash flows of a bond with associated weighting. In contrast, modified duration is a factor of the former in addressing price sensitivity to interest rate change. This is a very important adjustment for investors who wish to align their portfolio of bonds with interest rate expectations.

The process of calculating duration is straightforward, beginning with single bond calculations, and gradually includes additional complications like coupons and portfolio aggregations. The process helps not only to get an idea of what the individual bond is like but also how the bonds interact in the portfolio setting. The flexibility in controlling duration gives the investors the ability to make informed choices that suit their investment goals, especially in light of eventual changes in the policies or economic outlooks of the central banks that may result in the fluctuation of interest rates.

Convexity is an improved version of the analysis of how sensitive a bond is to price, where it takes into account the curvature of the price-yield curve. Duration provides a linear approximation; convexity considers that this relationship is not linear, in particular in the context of large movements of interest rates or bonds with embedded options. Convexity can be an especially important concept in highly volatile markets, as price changes are anything but linear, and valuations can vary enormously.

A calculation of the convexity is made by examining the second derivative of the price-yield relationship, which gives the causative factors with regard to how the length of a bond changes with the varying levels of yield. Positive convexity means that the price of a bond would increase by a higher level as the interest rate decreases, compared to the decrease in the price of the bond by the same interest rate increase. On the other hand, negative convexity, which typically appears on callable or mortgage-backed securities, implies that an increase in price does not occur as sharply as the decrease in price, resulting in special challenges and opportunities in portfolio management.

Investors can also use convexity to improve risk management plans and portfolio selection, and, as needed in optimizing risk management plans, investors can also select bonds that befit their risk tolerance and forecast the course of the market. To a greater degree, decision matrices will allow investors to approach uncertain rate environments by embracing the duration of the investing conditions in addition to the convexity, thus optimizing portfolios in terms of risk and gain.

In conclusion, it is quite clear to see that the concepts of duration and convexity are paramount in improving the way bond investors deal with the risk of interest rates. Such figures give vital information on how the prices of the bonds can respond to various movements in the rate of interest, and investors can make their decisions strategically that would help their portfolios and take advantage of the interest that may be in the market. A command of these ideas is what enables investors to approach bond markets with a sense of comfort and accuracy.

Credit Risk Assessment

In the world of bond investment, one ought to be very acquainted with the details of credit risk identification. Credit risk is the notion that the issuer of the bond will default on its obligations through non-payment of interest or repayment of the principal. The method to quantify this risk is quite diverse, as it starts with standard credit ratings and goes to more dynamic market indicators.

Credit ratings, which are delivered by agencies like Standard & Poor's, Moody's, and Fitch, give a glance at the credit rating of the issuer. These are classified as investment-grade and non-investment grade (or junk), with the former conferring that it has lesser risk and the latter the opposite. However, it is a mistake to consider these ratings only when making a decision. Ratings will give a snapshot assessment and may not necessarily show what is actually happening in the financial fitness of an issuer or the market situation.

In a bid to have a comprehensive outlook on credit risk, investors ought to take an in-depth, practical credit analysis. This entails an examination of the issuer's financial statements, with particular attention to the interest coverage ratio reflecting the issuer's capability to cover interest payments using earnings. A waning fraction can be an indication of impending problems. Further, qualitative variables relating to the stability of the management and trends in the industry should be taken into consideration. Acute management turnover or unpleasant trends in the issuer's industry can be a warning of upcoming troubles.

In addition to internal measures by the issuer, warning signals of credit weakening are available in market-based measures. Before a downgrade, there can be an expansion to credit spreads, which is an indicator that the market has shown greater perceived risk. In the same way, the price of credit default swaps (CDS), which is an insurance against default, may give some clue on how the market feels about an issuer and its ability to service its debt.

Investors need to be aware and keep alert on these indicators, as they need to always watch the indicators and move portfolios. The systematic process of monitoring the credit risk includes a checklist with quantitative and qualitative features. Such disciplined vigilance will help to assure investors that they can not only be prepared to face changes but can also become proactive to changes as opposed to reactive.

Use of scenario analysis in credit risk also enables an investor to have better control of the risk potential. With these simulations of different market conditions, e.g., shocks in interest rates or declines in some sectors, an investor may understand what effect it may have on his or her bond portfolio. This proactive means will facilitate strategic changes, e.g., rebalancing or hedging can be done in order to neutralise the risks identified.

In the end, it is a combination of the old style of analysis and what is going on in the markets that is required to analyze credit risks adequately. Through such a combination, investors are able to not only protect their portfolios against loss in case of defaults but also leverage the benefit of mispricing in the credit markets. This multi-faceted approach brings about a sense of preparedness among bond investors in relation to credit risk intricacies, which translates to high chances of earning returns without property loss.

Scenario Analysis for Risk Management

Scenario analysis is a crucial instrument in the sphere of risk management, particularly in the context of bond investments. This type of analysis takes into consideration the best theoretical market conditions applied to a portfolio of bonds so that investors can predict and plan the possible effects of the different financial environments. The ultimate aim is to perform a stress test on portfolios against future challenges that may occur in the financial markets, hence effectively managing risk proactively.

The scenario analysis process starts with the formulation of the parameters of the hypothetical scenarios. Such scenarios may be an interest rate shock where the interest rates increase or decrease rapidly, or a credit spread widening where significant shifts occur in the difference in returns between the bonds of different credit quality. With the understanding of these possible changes in the market, investors are now in a position to imagine and predict the performance of their portfolios with such bond products, albeit under various circumstances.

The development of the scenario analysis model needs a systematic procedure. Investors usually begin by choosing the most applicable situations to their portfolio and conditions at the time. An example is where an investor gambles to find out how a 200 basis point increase in interest rates would play out on interests in their portfolio. It is estimating how any such change will impact the value of all bonds in the portfolio in terms of factors such as duration and convexity, which determine sensitivity to changes in interest rates and movement in price, respectively.

After the scenario has been determined, it becomes necessary to simulate the effect the portfolio will receive. This can be achieved by means of financial modeling programs or tools such as Excel, which enable the computation of the possible alterations in portfolio value under every situation. The outcomes of such simulations indicate how these assets are most exposed to market changes and where the portfolio could use some modifications.

A number of strategic decisions can be made based on insights given by scenario analysis. For example, in a situation where it is identified that a portfolio is too highly exposed to interest rate risks, an investor may opt to restructure by trading long-term bonds with short-term bonds in order to bring down the duration of the portfolio. Correspondingly, in the case of a widening credit spread scenario, which points to the possibility that we are likely to see a worsening of credit, an investor may choose to rebalance the portfolio and lean on lower-rated bonds.

Scenario analysis is important in the continued risk management, in addition to providing a guide in making immediate portfolio corrections. This motivates investors to do regular scenario tests, applying templates and best practices that are adjusted to personal objectives and circumstances in the market. This constant monitoring has assisted in maintaining portfolios in line with the risk tolerance of investors, as well as maintaining the financial objective of the investors, even when the market environment changes.

Finally, the best way that any bond investor who wants to be on top of risk management can do so is through scenario analysis. Learning how to predict and prepare against market shocks gives the investor the chance of making sound decisions that can safeguard their investments during the unexpected events that happen in the market. The strategy will do more than make the portfolio resilient; it will also transform investors to feel more confident in tackling the bond market.

Hedging Techniques

When it comes to investing in bonds, hedging strategies are crucial in protecting portfolios against negative market fluctuations. Amid the complexities that the bond market entails, the application of derivatives and bond futures is a very important strategy among investors. These market instruments provide an avenue through which risks linked with interest rate fluctuations, as well as future credit exposures, can be reduced, hence creating stability and predictability of returns.

Hedging revolves around the concept and practice of different instruments, including Treasury futures, swaps, and credit default swaps. An example is the Treasury futures, which can enable an investor to hedge against interest rate risks because he/she is guaranteed the prevailing rates in the future. This may be especially useful during a period when interest rates are likely to increase, as it serves to adjust the value of the bond collection by counterbalancing the losses that it would assuredly experience due to the increase in the rates.

Swaps, however, offer a more customized method for handling the interest rate exposure. By means of interest rate swaps, the investors can continue to exchange floating rate obligations with fixed rate ones to stabilize cash flows and guard against fluctuating rates. Other potent devices include credit default swaps (CDS), which provide immunity against credit risk by bilateral division of the risk of default between the bondholder and the seller of the CDS.

Hedging strategy requires a cost-benefit analysis of the decision to hedge. The constraints imposed by the cost of realisation of these strategies, such as the fees of carrying out the strategies and the possible opportunity costs, have to be weighed against the risk deterrence advantage by the investors. The liquidity factor is equally core because the efficient entry and exit into positions may make a huge difference in terms of the efficiency of a hedge.

An effective illustration that can be used to show the concept of hedging is the application of Treasury futures as a control throughout a portfolio. Futures contracts can be used to adjust the duration of the portfolio to support the degree of exposure to interest rate risk held by the individual investor in relation to their attitude and view of the market. The active style will allow investors to have a certain amount of risk balance regardless of changes in the market.

Nonetheless, there are pitfalls associated with hedging. An example of a problem that can happen due to over-hedging is the emergence of excessive costs and low returns. The hedge may also be ineffective because of its basis risk, which occurs when the hedge is not perfectly related to the underlying exposure. Moreover, when using rather complicated instruments without a proper understanding, it is possible to face rather unjust outcomes, which is where the issue of complete knowledge and planning plays an important role.

In order to make a basic hedge successful, investors should follow a systematic flow right through position sizing, monitoring the hedge, and its unwinding. This includes questions of what the size of the hedge should be in relation to the exposure, the ongoing monitoring of market conditions, the performance of the hedge, and when it should be altered or closed out, given changes in the outlook of the market or the portfolio goals.

Essentially, hedging is a component of bond investment that cannot be ignored, as it offers the means of hedging against risks and offers portfolio strengthening techniques. With that knowledge and appropriate utilization of such techniques, investors are able to hedge their investments against the uncertainties of the market, making their investment process more even-ended and easier to predict.

Chapter 06: Portfolio Construction Strategies

Building a Bond Ladder

A bond ladder is a risk management tool in the world of fixed income investing that ensures it provides a consistent flow of income and includes the strategy of fighting against interest rate risk. The basis behind this investment process is to buy various bonds with varying maturities, which works to even out the reinvestment risk and smooth cash flows that are received over time. This is not only a stable method, but it will enable the investors to respond to the changes in the market conditions.

The main reason why a bond ladder is created is to generate a predictable income stream and, at the same time, reduce the risk posed by interest rate movements. An investor may also invest money in a set of bonds that have different maturity dates so that he or she is assured of a part of the investment maturing at regular intervals. The strategy means that the proceeds received on maturing bonds could be reinvested at the current market rates, which in a rising rate environment could be very beneficial.

The development of a bond ladder will start by determining the income requirement of an investor and the time frame. This step is important because it defines the general shape and height of the ladder.

Upon establishing such parameters, the selection of bonds with different maturities is followed. The choice of this should depend on risk tolerance, the target returns, and the market expectations of the investor.

The distribution of capital over the rungs of the ladder is a very important issue that should be carefully taken into consideration. The rungs indicate the type of bonds, and the bonds are set in a way whereby they mature on a chosen maturity date; hence, the capital is evenly distributed on such rungs to form a well-balanced portfolio. The distribution is useful in cushioning massive losses that may occur as a result of interest rate fluctuations or default of credit.

Monitoring and maintenance of the fulfilled ladder are also important to make it effective. This includes recording the composition of the ladder, monitoring the performance of individual bonds, and effecting a correction as markets change. Reinvestment strategies are very important in ensuring the integrity of the ladder since these strategies determine the utilization of proceeds of maturing bonds.

Building and maintaining a bond ladder is easy nowadays because modern technology provides tools and platforms that can make this task easier. Numerous brokerages offer ladder-building tools and portfolio graphical displays, which allow trading individuals to monitor their portfolios and make good choices easily. These tools are also useful when carrying out trades and when the ladder needs to be adjusted.

It is therefore not only a reliable source of income but also allows one to adjust to changes in the interest rates. Investors are able to achieve this by rolling up maturing bonds into new bonds with maturities comparable to the existing ones, so that there is an uninterrupted renewal of the portfolio along with emerging conditions in the market. Tax optimization and adaptation to rate changes will also help increase the performance of the bond ladder as a whole.

Basically, a bond ladder is an effective way of taking care of fixed-income investments. It is a trade-off between the necessity of income and the need to preserve capital, and it provides the opportunity to take advantage of the good market moments. The knowledge of the mechanism and advantages of the bond ladder will help investors become financially sounder and certain of their investments.

Barbell and Bullet Strategies

In the world of bond investing, two potentially interesting techniques are usually of interest to any investor who wants to be able to deal with the pathways of interest rates and the yield curve. These directions are called the barbell and the bullet approaches, having various approaches and possibilities of being useful depending on the investor's prospects and targets.

Barbell strategy can be defined by the fact that it is divided into two different stages of maturity: short-term and long-term bonds. This strategy successfully establishes a sort of barbell shape in the investor's portfolio by heavily weighting the portfolio at each end of the maturity scale and virtually nothing in the middle. The premise of such a strategy is to benefit from the liquidity and lower interest rate vulnerability of the short-term bonds without necessarily targeting the higher returns that characterize long-term securities. Use of the barbell strategy could also occur when the investors anticipate volatility in interest rates, with short-term bonds acting as a hedge against the uncertainty of interest rates rising as they are frequently due to maturity. One can reinvest the money back into the market, and in the long term, it acts as a gain as it will lock in higher rates over a greater period.

The bullet strategy, on the other hand, invests all the funds in bonds with one specific point of maturity. Investors with a target in mind, whether it is some kind of financial target like financing a child through college or covering a huge debt, might use this strategy to meet the particular target. This bullet process would reduce reinvestment risk and uncertainties since the maturities of the bonds would be matched with those of these future cash requirements. The policy is especially favorable in stable or declining interest rate scenarios where the investor can take advantage of bond holding to maturity without frequent portfolio tilt.

These two strategies come with advantages and possible disadvantages associated with them. This barbell strategy has padding and the possibility of optimization of yield by balancing short-range and long-range bond risk or returns. Nevertheless, it can carry an increased cost of transactions as well as the difficulty of operating two separate sections of bonds. Also, in flat yield curve settings, the difference between the yield of short-term and long-term bonds could be small, and this will lower the success of this strategy.

Conversely, the bullet strategy is less to handle and can offer peace-of-mind by keeping those investment maturities in alignment with a particular financial objective. However, it entails the risk of not being as flexible to market changes, as the single investor is very much dependent on a particular maturity date. If the interest rate goes up considerably, the worth of the bonds in a bullet strategy will fall, which will hurt the investor's ability to achieve their financial goals.

Ultimately, the decision between the use of barbell and bullet strategies depends on the market sentiment that an investor has, the risk appetite, and financial objectives. Barbell's strategy may provide better shelter and income possibilities in an environment where interest rates are anticipated to increase. On the other hand, a bullet strategy may give desired returns in times of rate stability or decrease to correspond to future cash flow requirements. These factors must be keenly followed by the investors when forming their bond portfolios so that they can follow their strategy or investment.

Diversification in Fixed Income

Fixed income investment diversification is part of risk management, and an improved returns strategy is based on diversifying investments in different sectors, credit quality, and maturities. The technique is especially vital in the case of a fixed-income portfolio to counter the negative event in any particular asset or market segment. The diversification strategy helps investors minimize portfolio exposure to any given shock and mitigate the variations in long-term returns.

Such is the distribution of sectors and issuers as one of the underlying principles of diversification in fixed income. This includes pooling of any form of bond, e.g., treasuries, investment grade corporates, high-yield, and municipal bonds, each with its risks and returns. This can be illustrated by the fact that government-backed treasuries tend to be listed as low-risk investments; however, they generally have lower returns than corporate bonds, which bear more credit risk and can potentially have better returns. Municipal securities offer a tax benefit, and that is why they are considered desirable in some portfolios, particularly to those in higher tax brackets.

Another dimension of diversification is credit quality. The inclusion of bonds with different credit ratings allows the investor to achieve a balance between portfolio risk and reward. Investment-grade bonds are bond investments that bring out stability and predictability, while high-yield bonds are riskier but tend to maximise returns. Determination of the creditworthiness of issuers is important because it directly influences the risk of default. Having a portfolio diversified in terms of issuer is also useful, in the sense that it allows the default of one issuer to have less of an effect on the overall results of the portfolio.

Bonds are diversified by maturity to reduce possible interest rate risk, which is known as maturity diversification of bonds. Short-term bonds are less sensitive to interest rate changes, so they offer stability; on the other hand, long-term bonds can offer better yields, although they are prone to interest rate changes. Through establishing a laddered portfolio, wherein the expiration times of bonds are staggered, investors will be able to find a balance between risk and return, and they have the means to do so since they would be able to reinvest as conditions in the market shift.

The use of international and emerging market bonds is yet another strategic layer known as global diversification. Such links will allow exposure to varying economic cycles and currency flows, which will offer geographic diversification. But at the same time, they come with some extra risks like currency risk and political instability, which should be handled.

Diversification can also be increased with the help of non-traditional bonds, like inflation-linked bonds or convertible bonds. TIPS are inflation-linked bonds that can be a hedge against the declining value of money. In contrast, the convertible bond has the upside potential of equities coupled with the downside cushion of fixed income investment.

The best portfolio management practice should entail continual monitoring and rebalancing as a way of enabling desirable diversification levels. Periodic portfolio rebalancing should help investors make sure that their sector and credit exposure are in line with their investment aspirations and risk tolerance. Rebalancing is either carried out on a calendar basis or in response to major movements in the market so as to ensure that the portfolio changes according to the different market conditions.

All in all, fixed income diversification is an active process encompassing the selection of the different types of bonds and their continuous handling. Diversification allows investors to attain a more robust portfolio, which is more prepared to bounce back from changes in the market and generate consistent returns by making investments spread across sectors, credit qualities, maturities, and geography.

Rebalancing Bond Portfolios

Here, a rigorous rebalancing discipline must be adhered to in order to sustain the targeted allocation and risk profile of a portfolio in the context of bond investing. This procedure is vital when an investor wants to realize his/her financial objective and acceptable level of risk in his/her portfolio. The rebalancing of bond portfolios refers to the process of equilibrating the allocation of the properties to remain on the target allocation, reacting to movements within the market conditions, and ensuring that the portfolio remains to suit the goals of the investor.

Rebalancing can be carried out in different ways, with each having its good and bad. Two of the standard approaches to rebalancing include calendar and threshold. The calendar-based rebalance is simple; investors establish a time of the year or period, e.g., annually or semi-annually, they review and rebalance their portfolios. This approach is simple in that it allows a fixed/scheduled process, which can prove very handy to individuals who are looking to adopt a systematic way of rebalancing.

Rebalancing Threshold-based rebalancing works with thresholds of deviation. Threshold-based rebalancing is so defined. It is a much more dynamic and responsive method to market changes since the method creates rebalancing only when required, and that may have the potential to cut down transaction costs. For example, a portfolio rebalance may occur when the bond sector's allocation differs more than 2% from its target level to make sure a portfolio is not too far away from its risk datum.

To achieve a good rebalancing strategy, one must know much about the goals of the portfolio, the risk tolerance of the investor, and the rebalancing cost. Taxes and transaction costs can have a large effect on the net returns of a portfolio; therefore, it is important to minimize the taxes and transaction costs. Investors need to be aware of the tax consequences of buying, selling, and rolling bonds because an impromptu tax bill could come with rebalancing.

One easily applicable strategy of rebalancing is to keep track of and monitor the performance of the portfolio and market situations now and then. At any rate, investors need to evaluate where they are invested, evaluate changes in the market, and make appropriate trades to keep their desired asset allocation. A checklist may come in handy here and assist an investor in the process of looking through the holdings, evaluating market changes, and enforcing trades efficiently.

In addition, with a combination of bonds with other asset classes, e.g., equities and alternatives, a portfolio can be diversified and the risk-adjusted returns maximised. The importance of bonds in a multi-asset portfolio is that they offer diversification, decrease volatility, and resolve particular investor objectives. Market outlook, age, and risk tolerance are some of the factors that need to be combined with strategic and tactical allocation decisions to maximize bond weights in the broader setting of the portfolio.

To sum up, this rebonding portfolio is a value-changing procedure that must be thought of critically through the objectives of the investor, market situation, and cost impacts. Through systematic rebalancing methods and sustaining a disciplined stance, investors can make sure that their investments will be well executed, align with their financial expectations, and eventually improve their overall chances of success in the long term.

Chapter 07: Tax Efficiency and Regulations

Taxable vs. Tax-Exempt Bonds

When it comes to bond investing, there are two very different types: taxable and tax-exempt, and two very different sets of consequences for the investor, especially in regard to matters of tax liability. It is important to understand the distinction between the two categories in order to make informed decisions based on one's financial objectives as well as the tax position.

Taxable bonds can either be corporate or Treasury bonds, where the interest income earned is taxable by the federal government. The state and local taxes may also tax this income, depending on the state of residence of the investor. This taxation can have implications on the net yield to be acquired by the investor, and it is necessary to figure out whether one is in a high tax bracket or a low tax bracket when investing in these bonds. The tax implications on the net yield of such bonds on the investor increase as the tax bracket in which the investor happens to be.

On the other hand, tax-exempt bonds, which are mainly municipal bonds, include a lot of tax benefits as they are usually exempt from federal taxes. These bonds also can be void of state and local taxes to investors living within the state where the bond is issued, which makes these bonds even more desirable. Municipal bonds are especially appealing to high-income investors who want to take maximum advantage of the lower-taxed interest. It is very important to mention, though, that not all municipal bonds will be totally tax-exempt. Those called private activity bonds may be subject to the Alternative Minimum Tax (AMT), so they can be less effective.

The investor should decide between the tax-exempt and taxable bonds based on their tax position. As an example, tax-exempt municipal bonds may be more advantageous to high-income investors as more after-tax earnings are possible in comparison with a taxable bond. On the other hand, the tax-exempt feature may not hold much utility to investors in lower tax brackets who may opt instead to invest in taxable bonds using the other available characteristics of the bond, including its yield or credit.

To calculate the benefit of the tax-exempt bond, investors estimate the taxable equivalent yield (TEY) that translates the yield of a tax-exempt bond into a taxable measure, so that the tax-exempt bond can be compared to a taxable bond. Since this calculation takes account of the tax rate of the investor, it calculates the break-even point at which a taxable bond would give the same after-tax yield as a tax-free bond. As an example, TEY at 4% municipal bond on a 35% tax bracket can be estimated to depict the successful pay when the taxes are estimated.

Tax-exempt bonds are not devoid of pitfalls despite the benefits they come with. One of the issues that investors should be careful of is when it is complex stuff, like the possibility of AMT exposure, as well as the tax consequences of various classes of municipal bonds. As an added measure, consideration should not be limited to tax aspects, but must also respect credit risk and market conditions with respect to the selection of tax-exempt bonds.

Conclusively, taxable and tax-exempt bonds are investments considered based on a keen analysis of the tax effect, personal finances, and investment objectives. Once aware of the peculiarities of every kind of bond, investors will be able to invest in a more relevant bond portfolio to their whole financial plans and be more tax-efficient and profit-efficient in general.

Calculating After-Tax Yield

The knowledge of the after-tax yield of the bond is very important to the investor when he/she want to make a more informed decision about the investment in a bond. Although the pre-tax yield gives a simple measurement of the expected returns, it does not consider the taxation credits paid that may drastically change the net income present in an investment. The after-tax yield enables the investor to compare different bonds in a more balanced manner, particularly when considering between taxable and tax-exempt securities.

In order to calculate the after-tax yield, the nominal yield of the bond should be known, which is the income that the bond earns an individual annually, and it regards the price of the bond as a percentage. This amount, however, does not indicate the amount to which the investor is actually left after deductions of the taxes. The first step is to take into account the tax bracket in which the investor falls, upon which the amount of tax that the investor will have to pay depends on the interest income earned.

To get a correct computation, tax impact should be computed at three levels, namely, federal, state, and local. All jurisdictions can have varying tax rates, and some types of bonds may enjoy tax-free status on any of the tax rates, like investment bonds. Much will have to be done in stages in order to perform these intricacies.

Calculate the federal tax liability in order to compute federal tax liability. In the case of a taxable bond, this means that the yield of the bond should be multiplied by the investor's federal tax rate. The result is the product of the yield that the federal taxes will take. This exercise may be skipped in the event that the bond is tax-free on the federal level, which is the case when it concerns municipal bonds.

Then come up with the state and local tax consequences. In some states, the tax exemption on bonds issued in that state takes place, whereas in other states, it does not happen. Investors must inquire as to whether the state has a special provision that may impose state tax. States imposing high rates of income tax can considerably influence the after-tax yield for the residents of such states.

To give a complete contrast, the cross-reference can be made to the after-tax yield, which is the ratio of the bond's pre-tax yield expressed as a percentage. Its calculation can be carried out by deducting the overall tax burden from the nominal yield and then dividing the outcome by the price of the bond. The yield after tax is calculated with the help of the formula:

After-Tax Yield = (Nominal Yield - Total Tax) / Bond Price

Practically, this formula enables investors to compare the net returns of two or more different bonds. A 5 percent corporate bond can easily be found appealing before the after-tax yield is computed, which comes out as higher than that of a municipal bond with a 3 percent yield.

Further, it is necessary to take into consideration the effects of capital gains taxes, where the capital gain taxes are applicable in case the sale of a bond before maturity fetches a profit. Any profit made on such a sale is liable to capital gains tax, which further affects the net revenue.

Lastly, investors must keep an eye out for special tax cases that may come along to change these calculations, including the Alternative Minimum Tax (AMT) or how Original Issue Discount (OID) bonds are treated. A thorough evaluation of all these aspects enables the investors to have a better grasp of actual returns on their investments and make better decisions in terms of investing in bonds.

Navigating Regulatory Changes

Regulatory amendments in the dynamic bond investing environment play a critical role in determining the course and results of investment planning. These reforms, which are sometimes considered too difficult and unwieldy, are very necessary to prevent manipulation of financial markets and shield investors. The reason why it is important to know these regulatory shifts, as pertains to bond investors, is because of the following: not only are these shifts essential to comply with, but in the process, it is imperative to take advantage of these changes.

Recent changes in regulations have brought about new demands and norms that immediately affect bond trading and investment. To buttress the fairness and transparency of bond markets, the Securities and Exchange Commission (SEC) has put in place processes that aim at making the bond markets more transparent. The criteria for securing best execution practices in retail bond trades now form one of the changes. This regulation requires brokers to make sure that the transaction of the trade is done in a way that maximizes the benefits according to the price, quickness of the transaction, and the probability of being able to execute the transaction. The effect on investors is a more transparent and competitive trading medium, which could result in improved prices and executions.

In addition to that, there has been a lot of evolution in disclosure and transparency requirements. The implementation of these rules has been important due to the role that the Financial Industry Regulatory Authority (FINRA) has played, especially in the implementation of Trade Reporting and Compliance Engine (TRACE). Price discovery in the bond market has moved toward TRACE reporting, which has made it easy to gain a better understanding of what is happening in the market and how pricing is trending. This increased transparency enables investors to make better decisions and align their portfolios in accordance with market advice and expectations.

Other areas where regulation has been introduced are regarding tax treatment and compliance. A change in tax laws and reporting standards by the Internal Revenue Service (IRS) can also affect the reporting of bond interest and capital gains and their taxation. As another example, taxpayer-related alterations in how tax-exempt bond proceeds have to be reported can affect the investors who use these tools to achieve tax efficiency as well. It is important to keep up with these changes since it will help maximize after-tax returns and ensure that tax obligations are met.

The best way that investors can overcome them is to make sure that they prepare resources and strategies that will enable them to think through them. It is also important to engage credible sources like the SEC, FINRA, and IRS, as real-time updates can be received and more knowledge related to regulatory changes may be gained. Alerts and specialist networks can also help investors change their plans as quickly as possible in response to new laws.

Besides updating themselves with the changes, investors ought to modify the composition of the portfolio to ensure it matches the changes in regulations. These may comprise further consideration of strategies that are compliance-oriented, such as documenting in order and being aware of the details of rules like the wash sale rule. Proper record keeping and the use of portfolio management software can help ensure that investors mitigate the risk of compliance and perform their trading procedures optimally.

The future of regulatory changes is all about being proactive. Regulatory challenges can be an opportunity with investors who remain at the top of the curve by always learning and using the resources offered by their profession. This would help them not only safeguard their investments but also be in a good position to make the most of the situation brought about by the changing regulatory trends that would see them gain a solid investment strategy in the bond market, which is resilient and compliant.

IRS Rules and Compliance

Bond investors who wish to remain compliant with the IRS and maximize their tax efficiency will be required to navigate the complex environment of IRS regulations. The Internal Revenue Service (IRS) has certain regulations that apply to the reporting and taxation of bond income, and such requirements can comprehensively affect the net returns of an investor.

The treatment of interest income is also critical to IRS regulations concerning bond investors. The interest that is accrued on bonds is normally viewed as taxable income. This income has to be properly declared by the investors in the tax returns; this can be done using forms like the 1099-INT, which indicates the amount of interest earned during a tax period. Also, if the interest income is above a specified limit, then Schedule B might be necessary. The issue of documentation and filing on time is the first and most important requirement to prevent fines and possible audits.

Another important rule that needs to be taken into account is the wash sale rule by the IRS, and bond investors should not disregard it. This rule does not allow investors to take a tax deduction on a security sold at a loss, provided that some essentially the same security is acquired within 30 days prior to or subsequent to the sale. This is because, to bond investors, it implies that repurchasing the same or a similar bond too soon after selling it at a loss may disallow the deduction of the loss. What does a "**substantially identical**" bond entail? The investors must keep all records of transactions in an orderly manner so that they can remain within the boundaries.

Daily traders and do-it-yourself (DIY) investors have to use an effective compliance method to remain on the positive side of IRS regulations. Maintaining detailed transaction records, using portfolio management tools, and being aware of changes in regulations are effective ways of evading the scrutiny of the IRS. The practices are not only useful in ensuring compliance, but they are also useful in ensuring tax efficiency due to the accuracy of gains and losses.

Malpractices in the area of compliance include the typical pitfalls that are rather costly. The most common ones are those that include late reporting or misstating the cost basis, and mischaracterizing income as capital gain instead. An example includes the purchase of a bond at a premium, followed by the subsequent sale of the bond without taking steps to reflect the change of its cost basis, which could lead to poor reporting of taxes. To avoid such errors in investor portfolios, investors should regularly examine their transactions and tax records to correct the errors in time.

Besides compliance, bond investors must stay updated regarding any changes in the regulations. Now and then, tax laws and reporting standards relative to interest and bond gains are modified by the IRS.

Being informed about these changes gives the investors a chance to strategise accordingly. The IRS site, financial news, and tax consultants should be good sources of information on these changes.

Nowadays, more than ever, managers need to be active in regulating portfolios of bond investors. Seeking reliable sources of information that can be updated in real-time, including the Financial Industry Regulatory Authority (FINRA), the IRS, and the Securities and Exchange Commission (SEC), may help one to monitor the development of new rules and responsible approaches. By complying with the rules established by the IRS, the risks can be avoided, and an investor will be able to understand how to optimize their taxes and ultimately reach their investment goals more confidently.

Chapter 08: Advanced Bond Instruments

High-Yield Bonds and Due Diligence

Junk bonds are also high-yield bonds that introduce an unusual risk in the fixed income market. These bonds are differentiated from their investment grade potential in that their credit rating is not at or above the standard required by major rating agencies like Standard & Poor's, Moody's, and Fitch. Companies issuing high-yield bonds are typically those in businesses where there is a great deal of leverage and consequently higher risk, and the issuing of high-yield bonds is usually a resource to finance an expansion or to refinance old debt.

The attraction of high-yield bonds to investors is the possibility of earning higher returns than traditional bonds. There is, however, greater default and volatility risk associated with this, and in many respects, the performance of these bonds will be closely linked to the performance of equity markets. As the past evidence demonstrates, high-yield bonds may have a high rate of returns, yet, at the same time, they are characterized by higher rates of defaults compared to investment-grade bonds. The link to equities suggests that the high-yield bonds can be more volatile -- especially in times of downturns in the economy.

It is always important to conduct due diligence prior to investing in high-yield bonds. It is done by looking at the financial health of the issuer, risks associated with the sector, and the quality of management. Investors need to analyze financial statements in order to determine whether an issuer will fulfill its debt. Financial stability is indicated by key ratios such as cash flow, debt ratio levels, and interest cover ratios. It is also necessary to know the risk profile of the industry because some are more prone to economic or regulatory fluctuations.

The terms and conditions of the bond agreement, i.e., bond covenants, have to be looked into closely. These covenants may have provisions that shield the bondholders by limiting other actions of the issuer, like raising new debt or disposing of assets at large. Learning about these covenants may allow investors to avoid red flags in an investment, including so-called zombie companies, which are firms that depend on debt to stay in business and are likely to default in case of deterioration of the economic situation.

High-yield bonds have a strategic aspect relating to diversification of an investment portfolio. Nevertheless, investors should expose themselves to a fixed income allocation as a way of offsetting risks. The risks of issuer and industry diversification can prevent the concentration of effects caused by bond defaults of individual issuers. Risk can be further controlled through position sizing regulations and integration of high-yield bonds with other forms of fixed-income funds.

When high-yield bonds are involved, investors ought to also take cognizance of the macro environment. When one finds himself in an economic recovery phase, the bonds get to enjoy better credit terms and more investor risk tolerance. On the other hand, in a falling market, they can be adversely affected since the risks in the form of defaults can increase.

To sum up, high-yield bonds can be a good source of attractive returns, but appropriate due diligence and planning to integrate them into the portfolio can be considered. High-yield bonds are an alluring investment opportunity, and with proper analysis of financial health, evaluation of risks associated with a particular sector, and strict use of the concept of diversification, an investor can enjoy the benefits of such high-yield bonds without worrying about the threats that accompany them.

Mortgage-Backed Securities

MBS is a fundamental point in the history of modern financial markets, as it is the only combination of housing finance and the rest of the bond market. This grouping together of many mortgage loans is the way that these securities are produced, and they are subsequently sold as bonds to investors. A basic structure of an MBS is determined by tranches through which different cash flows are allocated to investors depending on the level of risk and reward that the investor is willing to receive. Tranching will enable the investors to choose the tranche that corresponds to their risk appetite in the first tranche of losses that will be suffered by the first tranche to the least exposed.

The charm of MBS is the fact that they generate a moderately steady revenue base based on mortgage repayments. These payments are normally transmitted to investors as a monthly repayment of both interest and capital. The nature of such cash flows can be very different depending on the nature of mortgages and the prevailing interest rate environment.

The most vital thing about investing in MBS is that one needs to be aware of the risks associated with prepayment, extension, and so on. The prepayment risk occurs when homeowners pay off their mortgages before their due dates, especially during a rapidly falling interest rate environment, whereby it is likely that they will refinance. This can result in the unexpected acceleration of the repayment of principal, and investors might be required to reinvest in lower prevailing rates, which may hurt the overall returns. On the other hand, there is extension risk; extension risk is experienced where there is an increase in interest rates, thereby slowing down prepayments due to a lack of refinancing. This could increase the period of security longer than anticipated, and this would expose investors to interest rate risks since they have kept the security over a long period.

The quality of the mortgage pool that the MBS is secured to, the quality of the servicer managing the loans, and the structure of the specific deal will all be part of the evaluation process to assess the quality of the MBS to include them in the portfolio. Owned or guaranteed agency MBS, e.g., those issued by Fannie Mae or Freddie Mac, tend to be backed by government-sponsored organizations, and this adds an implicit guarantee to the MBS. However, non-agency MBS does not include the mentioned type of guarantees, which makes a credit risk analysis more demanding.

Other factors that investors should consider include the aspects of liquidity, minimum investment requirements, and availability through different products such as mutual funds or exchange-traded funds (ETFs). Some of the risks in individual securities may be overcome, and the securities may be diversified through BS ETFs and mutual funds with more compact investments in BS and more direct access points to the retail investor.

The performance of MBS is pivotal in the macroeconomic set-up. The interest rate direction, the state of the housing market, and the pace of the economy can also have a potent influence on the rate of mortgage default, as well as the prepayment rates, which affect the returns on MBS. Therefore, it is very important to be aware of economic indicators and movements in the mortgage market when it comes to MBS investing as well.

On the whole, mortgage-backed securities are an attractive tool to income-oriented investors who require exposure to the housing segment in a bond format. The difficulty and nature of risks involved in the securities, however, need to be understood well and considered carefully in the overall context of an investment portfolio approach maintained by the investor.

Inflation-Protected Bonds and FRNs

TIPS, also called inflation-protected bonds, and FRNs are special securities created to help protect the investor against inflation and fluctuation in interest rates. These bonds provide an exciting option to investors who want to stretch their money in different angles and take care of liabilities in the medium term, over inflation, and instability in interest rates.

TIPS are a form of U.S Treasury security designed to ensure investors are not affected by inflation. Their major value would readjust based on the alterations in the Consumer Price Index (CPI), which is one of the major indicators of inflation. This adjustment will mean that the buying power of the principal of an investor does not erode with time. TIPS is designed to benefit from an increasing rate of inflation, as it implies the growth of the principal loan increases and increases interest payments as the established coupon rate is applied to the increasing value of the lent principal sum. It is this mechanism that renders TIPS a useful instrument for investors who foresee an inflationary situation in the economy.

However, floating rate notes (FRNs) save on the inflation of interest rates. In contrast to the traditional fixed-rate bonds, interest payments on FRNs are readjusted every three months and are done according to a reference interest rate, such as the fed funds rate or the LIBOR (London Interbank Offered Rate). This quality enables the FRNs to trade at such a stable value when interest fees rise, which is a hedge against a fall in the price of bonds, which usually comes along with rising interest rates.

The combination of TIPS and FRNs can present a good balance in activity between the risks of coping relatively with inflation and interest. TIPS can only be favorable when inflation is unexpected in spikes, as part of the protection of the true value of investments. FRNs, on the contrary, perform best where interest rates are projected to increase, as they may yield higher returns as opposed to fixed-rate bonds.

Nevertheless, some considerations should not be disregarded by the investors when investing in these instruments. The major hazard of using TIPS is the phantom income problem. When the inflation rises, the value of the TIPS also increases because the interest is adjusted to the inflation rate. Still, when the period of inflation ends, the scenario becomes different because the investors end up being taxed. However, they are yet to receive the interest they should have received during inflation. This may end up being a greater tax liability without the current cash being used up by benefits. Although RNs eliminate the interest rate risks, they receive lower returns than fixed-rate bonds in a stable or dropping interest rate regime. They thus are not attractive in a stable or dropping interest regime.

Access to TIPS and FRNs is comparatively easy, going through different sources like auctions, exchange-traded funds (ETFs), and mutual funds. These financial products form part and parcel of the fixed income market that enables investors to customize their portfolio on the basis of interest rate and inflation expectations. It is through the exploitation of these bonds that investors would have a more robust portfolio that could easily stand up against economic uncertainties.

Incorporating TIPS and FRNs into one portfolio needs to be factored into the demographics of what is happening in the whole financial bucket, and also needs to be factored into the goals that you, as a particular individual, have set for yourself. Studying the peculiarities of the said instruments, their tax treatment, and the current situation on the market is important to maximize their advantages. TIPS and FRNs can add defensive qualities to a portfolio, providing security against the pressure of inflation and fluctuations of interest rates; in the right mix, they help the portfolio sleep soundly at night.

Green Bonds and ESG Considerations

The introduction of green bonds is set to change the fixed income market by ensuring that they are used to finance environmentally friendly projects. Issued often by governments, corporations, or even financial institutions, these bonds are purely dedicated to be used in sustainability-promoting projects and have the proceeds of such bonds sanctioned towards such initiatives only. This involves investments in renewable energy, energy efficiency, pollution prevention, and sustainable agriculture, among others. Some frameworks that have brought about the emergence of green bonds include the International Capital Market Association (ICMA) Green Bond Principles, which guide the use of proceeds, project evaluation, and reporting.

The theme of green bonds was on the rise as more investors tried to make their portfolios green, addressing environmental, social, and governance (ESG) factors. ESG is now part of investment decisions, and this trend of sustainable investing has increased in scope. The trend has been spurred by the increasing awareness of the long-term dangers of environmental degradation and social injustices, as well as the possibility of having sustainable projects that generate good competitive returns.

The increasing popularity of ESG in fixed income marketplaces can be attributed to the fact that the issuance of green bonds is on the rise worldwide. Although these instruments attract investors due to their environmental positivity, they also attract investment because they fall within the sustainability domain. The same has happened to green bonds as they have gained demand; there has been an increased scrutiny of their legitimacy as well. When investing in green bonds, investors should pay keen attention to the transparency and reporting of green bond issuers to avert the risk of being victims of greenwashing, which happens when the funds are incorrectly labeled as green initiatives.

Green bonds should be evaluated by taking into account the projects they fund and the criteria according to which they became certified. The investors ought to look at clarity in reporting by the issuer, soundness of third-party certification, and the effects of the funded projects in terms of the environment. Transparency must be practiced so that it will be clear that the proceeds are genuinely going towards realizing environmental sustainability.

It is not just the inclusion of green bonds into bond portfolios that involves incorporating ESG considerations. Investors will have to weigh the quest to make a good environmental impact against the conventional measures of risk and returns. This necessitates going into portfolio building with delicate discernment, as investors consider the costs and benefits of achieving good ESG impact and earning monetary returns. The strategies can involve constructing ESG-titled portfolios where focus is placed on bonds of issuers having robust sustainable operations, and the risk-reward profile of each investment deserves to be considered.

The green bond and ESG-labeled debt markets are constantly growing, and investors are now better armed to make sound decisions on their investments. This entails access to ESG ratings, impact reports, and frameworks that can be used to appraise sustainability metrics. Incorporating ESG into their investment processes, investors also have an opportunity to invest in a more sustainable future and work on achieving financial goals.

Another indication of a monumental paradigm transform is the birth of green bonds and the integration of ESG factors in bond investing in fixed income securities. It demonstrates an emerging understanding of how the investments can contribute to such global issues as climate change and social inequality. With such a trend, green bonds are expected to take center stage in sustainable investing, where investors can invest their money in green bonds in a bid to maximize their returns and at the same time have a positive impact on the environment.

Chapter 09: Bond Funds and ETFs

ETFs vs. Individual Bonds

When it comes to fixed income investments, the difference between Exchange-Traded Funds (ETFs) and individual bonds is crucial when investors need to match their objectives of investing to their financial targets. Both alternatives present unique benefits and pitfalls, each one of them needing to be analyzed discerningly in terms of cost, liquidity, and transparency.

Exchange-Traded Funds (ETFs) offer an opportunity to buy a diversified portfolio of bonds without the need to invest in single securities. This diversification is part and parcel of the nature of ETFs, which combine investment by pooling together to hold a large collection of bonds, thereby diluting risk across issuers and asset sectors. Because of the mechanics of the operations of ETFs, these securities can be priced and traded on a daily basis like stocks, giving investors the ability to make transactions on the major exchange intraday. Such liquidity can be beneficial, especially at a time when the market is experiencing volatile dynamics, since it allows investors to get in or out of a position quite conveniently.

Compared to other investments, ETFs tend to have simple cost structures, and expense ratios are well-disclosed. The investors should, however, be aware of other expenses where there may be a spread between the bid-ask, and some transaction fees may be charged as part of the process. Nevertheless, ETFs can have hidden expenses, but this trade can be appealing to investors who want to access a general market position with ease of administration and the efficiency of a single factor.

On the other hand, when an investor invests in individual bonds, there are other advantages and factors. Individual bonds: Individual bonds enable the investor to have direct ownership, where one has exact control over maturity dates, timing of interest payments, and the exact nature of the credit quality of the issuers. This form of customization is especially attractive to people with specialized cash flow requirements or who desire a specific approach to investing, e.g., retirees who require regular income.

Liquidity is, however, an issue with individual bonds. Unlike ETFs, which trade in exchanges, individual bonds are generally traded over the counter, and this may lead to increased bid-ask spreads and therefore poor price transparency. The absence of liquidity may be especially acute in calm times of market turmoil, and it may mean that selling bonds rapidly without affecting the price is not easy.

In the process between ETFs and individual bonds, investors have to consider trading benefits in terms of diversification and liquidity advantages, characteristics that come with holding ETFs against the benefits of control and customization that come with holding individual bonds. The determination tends to depend on the particular objectives, risk tolerance, and relative significance of factors attributable to the investor, such as the predictability of income and the presence of market accessibility.

Depending on the priorities, ETFs might be the most attractive option, as they have the conveniences of ease of access and diversification, stock-like trade capabilities, and flexibility with bond investments. In contrast, portfolios that hold single bonds can be more appropriate to investors, who attach importance to the flexibility and customization of their investments to fit discrete financial objectives.

However, they come at the expense of liquidity and transparent cost structures.

After all, the choice of using ETFs or individual bonds in the end is not universal. It involves a careful study of his/her financial goals, economic factors in the market, and the nature of the investment vehicles in question. The investors should carefully assess these factors to come up with informed decisions that correlate with the overall investment strategies. The portfolio of the investor can be strategically positioned to understand the dynamics of the bond market.

Mutual Funds and Closed-End Funds

Mutual funds and closed-end funds are two related, but fundamentally different bond investing vehicles that have their benefits and issues that can be brought to an investor. A type of fund that can be easily sold and repurchased is a mutual fund, which is typically unconstrained, and investors can purchase and liquidate the shares according to the net asset value (NAV) that is determined at the end of the day. This is one of the most attractive aspects of mutual funds, as it allows liquidity where investors have the freedom to both get in and out of their investments comparatively easily. However, this liquidity is accompanied by the requirement of managing the inflows and outflows on the part of the fund manager, which can, at times, affect the investment strategy and returns.

In contrast, closed-end funds (CEFs) do not work in the same manner. They release a specific number of shares in an initial public offering, and these are treated like stocks or stock entities that go into the stock market. This form enables CEFs to utilize leverage more efficiently, borrowing funds in order to increase the returns, because they are not compelled to deal with daily redemptions. Such leverage is, however, capable of increasing losses as well, and, hence, CEFs are riskier investments.

Mutual funds and CEFs are similar in that they both are vehicles where money is pooled between different investors to diversify in a portfolio of bonds, providing professional management skills and diversification advantage that may otherwise be hard for average individual investors to do themselves. These funds offer diversification, which allows for reducing the risk, since the investment can be diversified across types of bonds, maturities, and credit ratings.

The most important difference between the two is their price and trading. Although mutual funds are always quoted at the NAV, CEFs can only be quoted at their NAV during a wide range of market prices throughout the trading day as dictated by the supply and demand of capital, and, unlike an ETF, as a result, CEFs often trade at prices greater than their NAV or a discount (often at significant amounts) to the NAV. This is another pricing dynamic that makes CEFs even more complex, as the pricing is based on more than the underlying assets; it is also based on the sentiment and volume of trading.

There is also a difference in expense ratio between the two types of funds. Because of active management and liquidity maintenance expenses, mutual funds usually have higher levels of expense ratios. Although CEFs are also actively managed, they can be cheaper on an expense ratio basis than a mutual fund, but leverage and trading fees can make the difference in terms of overall returns.

Investors have to take such considerations with regard to their risks and investment objectives. Mutual funds may therefore be interesting to those who want a simple and easy-to-liquidate and exchange investment in bonds. In contrast, CEFs may draw the attention of those who want to have potentially larger returns and are willing to take the risks. The decision to invest in mutual funds or CEFs all comes down to the investment strategy of the individual consumer, whether they seek the most liquid and stable investments or are intending to risk more in the hopes of getting a higher reward.

When deciding between these options, a factor that investors should consider is also the tax implications, in that both types of funds have tax implications that differ, subject to the type of bond the fund holds. The knowledge of these quirks can significantly affect the net returns on such investment vehicles.

Essentially, mutual funds and closed-end funds can be a great opportunity for bond investors, with each of them providing its pros and culminating risks. Investors will be able to make informed decisions when they know the structures of these funds, how their prices work, and the riskiness of the funds to fit in their financial goals.

Hidden Risks in Pooled Products

These risks are often less apparent and are present in the world of pooled fixed income products, where a number of different risks are relatively transparent compared to holding them in an individual bond. These risks are either latent or obvious, but they are very important in determining the performance of investments such as bond funds and ETFs. The structural risk of such pooled vehicles is one of the major issues of concern. This is in terms of the liquidity match, which is a mismatch between the liquidity of funds' shares and the liquidity of assets. The difference may create serious problems when the markets are under pressure, as during the March 2020 market crunch, when bond ETFs were dislocated and under a discount on net asset value (NAV).

The other vital factor is the redemption risk, which is very crucial in open-ended funds. Shareholders are free to withdraw investment on any day, and this may prompt fund managers to sell off the assets, even at undesirable prices, to raise funds to respond to redemptions. Such can initiate a run on the fund, which further substantiates market turbulence and might still result in extra NAV inconsistencies.

Besides, the credit, maturity, and leverage risks of the underlying portfolio can be hidden by pooled products. The format of the fund can enhance these dangers, resulting in undesirable consequences for the investors. As an example, a bond fund sold with a stable value designation may show substantial duration drift when interest rates are spiking, so as to cause a mismatch between investor expectations and the realized performance figures.

There is a considerable risk of index tracking error and portfolio transparency gaps as well. A bond ETF may also underperform its index because investors can use a bond ETF that is not exactly a perfect replica of the index. Such tracking error may be especially explicit in high-yield bond ETFs, where the liquidity situation is more restricted and transaction expenses are greater.

Investors are advised to review the fund holdings and liquidity statistics on a regular basis to temper the risks. The risk in question may be identified by knowing about the fund, the strategy of the fund, the fluidity of its assets, and how the fund would perform in market-stressed situations in the past. Also, investors cannot go wrong with keeping open lines of communication with fund managers so that they are aware of any changes in strategic direction or market environment that could produce a difference in their investment.

To conclude, pooled fixed income investments have received attention due to their ability to cause diversification and convenience in handling. However, they have risks to be considered and monitored as well. Knowing of these invisible dangers, investors will be able to make better decisions that can be in line with their risk tolerance and financial objectives.

Evaluating Fund Managers

In order to get an effective judgment of fund managers, an in-depth study must be conducted, evaluating them on the basis of their performance indicators, strategies, and historical effectiveness. Investors must be equipped with the necessary tools and knowledge to determine the capacity and performance of fund managers in the acute environment of bond investments.

The starting point that is of crucial importance in the evaluation process is what kind of performance measures a manager should use to identify a manager as having skills. Alpha, Sharpe ratio, and information ratio are metrics that give an idea of the risk-adjusted performance that a manager can attain. Alpha compares the excess return of a fund against a benchmark, indicating what value was added by the manager's investment decision. At the same time, the Sharpe ratio measures the risk-adjusted performance by dividing the portfolio mean by the portfolio standard deviation by the risk-free rate. The information ratio expands on this by dividing the excess portfolio return by the volatility of the excess portfolio returns, providing a more meaningful analysis of consistency in the performance.

On top of the available quantitative measures, it is important to know the investment approaches of a manager. This includes the ability to know the type of management style (passive or active) and the top-down or bottom-up approaches taken by a manager. Passive management is usually employed where a benchmark index is replicated, and the process aims to realize a similar level of performance to the index. On the contrary, active management aims to beat the benchmark in strategic decisions. A top-down approach relies on macro factors to drive investment strategy, whereas the bottom-up strategy places importance on the individual security selection based on company fundamentals.

It is another critical area of study because funds are evaluated based on their performance over past periods. Investors should examine the historical track record information to differentiate the profit that is made due to skill as opposed to the profit born of luck. This is associated with performance attribution analysis through which investors can break down the returns into determinants of repeatable strategies and those of a one-off occurrence. As an example, rotation to different sectors may signify strategic prowess, whereas individual credit bets may signify opportunistic success.

Due diligence is a part and parcel of fund manager evaluation. Investors ought to have checklists with questions on the length of the manager, their investment process, and risk controls. The duration of the manager's tenure is important as it gives an idea of their experience and stability. In contrast, the investing process should show how systematic the decision-making of the manager is. Risk controls indicate how managers take care of the risks that could lead to losses, therefore demonstrating their resilience to market volatility.

The red flags are also tools to be used in examining the fund managers. These may include regular alterations of the investment strategy, discrepancies between performance results and the peers, and the absence of transparency in communication. Being aware of these red flags, investors will be able to prevent certain traps.

Before concluding, this approach should be considered in terms of looking deterministically at both quantitative indicators and qualitative analysis to ascertain the level of fund manager efficiency. Investors can therefore make an informed decision when they are deciding what fund managers to invest in, as the three aspects have been vetted carefully to suit their financial objectives and risk tolerance. Such a thorough review also helps in choosing competent fund managers and improving the entire investment approach, as financial targets can only be achieved with the assistance of the ability to cooperate with competent fund managers.

Chapter 10: Tools and Resources for Bond Investors

Digital Tools for Bond Analysis

In the new environment of bond investing, online stock tools have been revealed to be crucial to both first-time and experienced bond investors. The tools provide an efficient way of analyzing, managing, and optimizing bond portfolios and make the complex environment of fixed income more approachable and actionable. Investors can effectively harness the use of technology to ease their way through the complexities involved in bond investing, including bond price as well as computation of yield, risk, and portfolio management.

Among the main digital instruments that can be used to analyze bonds are the spreadsheet-based programs such as Microsoft Excel. Elaborate features in Excel enable investors to perform complex bond valuations coupled with yield computation easily. With the help of pre-defined functions like PRICE and YIELD, investors get the opportunity to calculate the present value of bonds and their expected returns over various intervals of time. These functions help to make calculations of the fair value of a bond in terms of its coupon, maturity, and general interest rates in the market very easy. Also, Excel is flexible, so investors can develop formulas and models that suit a particular investment scenario and perform scenario analysis and stress testing.

Other than using spreadsheets, online bond calculators are useful tools in the calculation of a bond investment, and online bond platforms are an interactive means of calculating the bond investment. Finding bonds: FINRA has developed a bond center that allows easy searching of issues based on credit rating, yield, and maturity, among others. Morningstar has developed a Bond Screener that is usable by all. Most of these platforms can be linked to real-time market data, and investors will have an opportunity to make informed decisions based on the current status in the market. Furthermore, there are tools with visualization capabilities that assist an investor in grasping the dynamics between price and yield, as well as how a change in interest rates affects the prices of bonds.

The other major development in the area of digital tools used to analyze bonds is the increase in mobile apps. These apps offer investors the comfort of accessing bond market data and tools of analysis when they are not at their work desks. Most of these applications are made to operate with synced desktop platforms, where there is a seamless experience between the two devices. Also, mobile applications frequently have alerts and notifications, notify investors about certain events on the market, and new potential opportunities.

Digital tools play an essential role when risk management is done on bond portfolios. Risk analytic software solutions provide information on such statistics as duration, convexity, and credit risk. These two tools are being used by investors to quantify how their portfolios respond to the movement in interest rates and to determine whether they have any weaknesses in their bonds. Investors will have an easier time making hedge decisions and portfolio adjustments since they have a more comprehensive account of risks and their presentation in a visual format.

Moreover, there is a new trend to combine artificial intelligence and machine learning with tools in the analysis of bonds that changes how investors think about bonds. These technologies allow the large volume of market information to be processed, and new patterns and trends that cannot be easily discerned by traditional methods are identified. The predictive analytics, which AI-powered tools can deliver, will also provide investors with insight in advance on what to expect in the market and any possible risks in the investment.

In conclusion, technology is a game-changer when it comes to the analysis of bonds and how investors carry out the analysis. These tools give investors the power to make better and more sure decisions in the confusing world of bond buying. They supply the investor with complete data, analytical abilities, and intuitive interfaces. Technology is likely to keep improving, which means that the ability of digital tools to enable bond analysis will increase and help investors in reaching their financial objectives even more effectively.

Leveraging Peer Communities

Peer communities are a good source of information and guidance for investors in the world of bond investors who are interested in gaining more information and making sensible decisions. These groups of people you will see on various forums, social media pages, and also local investor groups where members share ideas, relay and discuss their strategies, as well as get the latest feedback amongst groups of fellow investors. When investors involve themselves in these communities, they are able to extract a bigger pool of knowledge, which in most cases is more dynamic and practical than financial writings.

Participation in peer groups enables investors to keep abreast with the current trends and changes in the bond market. These sites are also likely to have an exchange of ideas about the prevailing conditions in the markets and other factors, such as new products in the markets and changes in regulation that are likely to affect investment plans. Through connections to others in the market who are actively participating in the market, the investors will be able to learn varied views and experiences of different people. Such an exchange of knowledge can also be of great help to those who are new to the world of bond investing and are still exploring the ins and outs of bond investing.

Also, peer communities provide another type of unique opportunity to investors, which allows asking questions and getting answers from a person who has some first-hand experience. Whether they need to know more about the subtle nature of bond pricing, what form of bonds exist, and what risks are tied to specific investments, these communities offer a medium of open communication and constant education. The investors are in a position to consult portfolio structure, risk management, and other important aspects of bond investing, thus improving their decision-making process.

One more strong point of using peer communities is their opportunity to get in touch with real-time insights and market intelligence. As opposed to stationary knowledge in textbooks or reports, the dynamics of these communities describe the vibe in the market and the new tendencies. The investors will have the advantage of getting up-to-date information on the interest rate fluctuations, the economic indicators, and geopolitical events that will affect the bond market. This speed in terms of informational access enables the investors to update their strategies in a timely manner and reap benefits in the market.

In addition, investors who are members of a peer community feel a sense of solidarity and support. The great thing about bond investing is that it is a very individual thing, but it is good to surround oneself with people who understand. Investors are capable of discussing their gains and setbacks, celebrating victories, and receiving reminders of how, through group effort, they can reach financial goals. This friendly atmosphere can help an investor feel confident, especially when fluctuations in the market occur or uncertainty arises, where investors might be in need of reassurance and counseling.

To sum up, it is possible to say that peer community integration in the bond investing process has a lot of advantages that can increase the knowledge, confidence, and success of investors. Engaging in such communities will allow investors to have all the available information at their disposal, keep up with the current events and changes in the market, and gain insights and advice based on other people's experiences. Neither newcomers who want to know more about investments, nor more experienced investors, who need to understand how to improve their investment tactics, can do without peer communities, which complement the existing tools and help them learn even more.

Ongoing Learning and Education

It is in this continually changing bond investment landscape where education and active learning are very essential in keeping the investor updated and well-skilled to cope with the intricacies of the market. The volatility of the financial market, driven by indicators of the state of the economy, regulatory changes, and financial product innovation, requires stakeholders of the industry to attach importance to lifelong learning by both first-time investors and those with experience.

Investors are advised to use the force of online resources, which provide an ocean of information and applications to boost their knowledge level in the bond market. Sites, applications, and calculators like the FINRA bond center and Morningstar bond screener offer much-needed information and analysis tools, allowing investors to research and screen Bond investments in a comprehensive manner. These platforms are the gateways of real-time data, which enables the investor to remain updated on the trends in the market and make their decisions based on their knowledge.

In addition to digital tools, enrolling yourself in peer groups may help tremendously in adding valuable insights to an investor and his/her choice of strategy. Online sites and internet communities such as Bogleheads.org and investing on the Reddit social media platform allow unmediated real-time discussions and peer sharing. Through these communities, there is a medium of discussion and Q&A, as well as a sharing of strategies, where collective intelligence works well.

Keeping abreast of the latest strategies, product innovation, and regulatory changes is also vital in ensuring that one maintains a competitive advantage in bond investing. Investors are urged to subscribe to highly rated podcasts, newsletters, and webinars that concentrate on fixed income and market trends. These materials offer well-selected materials and professional conclusions, so investors have all the necessary information about the changes that may have implications for their portfolio.

In order to create a sustainable self-improving system, the idea about the necessity to establish unambiguous goals of learning, monitoring, and assessing newly obtained information with regard to credibility deserves to be put forward. This formulated process not only boosts knowledge acquisition status but is also useful in transferring new knowledge regarding the practical application of new strategies and concepts.

Additionally, stockholders ought to adopt an initiative methodology of stock examination and management. It is pivotal to conduct regular portfolio reviews, either quarterly or on the occasion of a significant event, and align the investment strategies with the current market environment. These reviews ought to be performed with checklists that assess performance, exposure to risks, and compatibility with the financial objectives.

The act of continuing education and learning when it comes to bond investing is not a suggestion but a requirement in the contemporary financial world. With the help of online apps and tools, participation in peer groups, and subscriptions to learning services, investors can create a solid learning environment from which they can thrive throughout their lives. Such a foundation enables them to adapt to changes in the market, to be critical in evaluating new products, and to optimize their position so that they invest successfully in the long run.

Building a Lifelong Learning System

This particular environment of bond investing is constantly changing, and being on top of the game and staying flexible is crucial in keeping pace. To remain successful in the bond market, the investor must come up with an effective lifelong learning system that helps the investor understand the market in all aspects. This not only entails garnering the basics but also constantly upgrading the understanding of the current happenings in the economy, with regard to regulations and new financial innovations taking place.

An effective way of developing such a system is by establishing precise goals of learning that will suit his/her investment strategy. This information should determine the topics that the investors want to know more about, such as the macroeconomic indicators, types of bonds, or advanced strategies. It is possible to develop a systematic learning plan with quantifiable goals that will help monitor the process and guarantee positive changes.

Electronic tools are of crucial importance in this lifelong learning experience. The internet is flooded with a myriad of tools and sites that expose one to new information and professional views. Websites, applications, and calculators aimed at analysing bonds may be useful for conducting research and making choices. Example: The FINRA Bond Center or the Morningstar Bond Screener are all platforms with analytics and an in-depth amount of data that can assist the investor in weighing an investment decision and monitoring the market.

What other activities may be valuable besides using digital tools? Being involved with peer communities can be of great help. There are online community forums and social investing networks like Bogle-heads.org or Reddit r/investing that allow investors to interact with one another, pose inquiries, and exchange experiences. Such societies breed community intelligence so that players can acquire a wide range of views and a real-time insight into changes in the market.

It is essential to stay up to date with the emergence of new strategies, products, and regulations in order to have a comprehensive overview of the bond market. To continuously learn, one can subscribe to industry newsletters, listen to podcasts, and attend webinars to obtain a better understanding of upcoming trends. Such sources are usually accompanied by professional reviews, interviews, and discussions that can enrich knowledge on a complex matter and find technical solutions to changes that are taking place in the market.

Quite another important part of the lifelong learning system is the evaluation of new information that concerns the question of its credibility. The investor has to enhance the ability to determine the reliability of sources of information and the validity of information that is being consumed. Cross-checking information, looking at bias, and referring to more than one source could make the decisions more accurate and provide a wide range of information.

In order to support such a process of constant learning, the development of a personal knowledge bank can be very productive. This could also consist of an online resource of articles, research papers, and notes that could be easily referred to and updated. Thanks to the systematic organization of information, it is possible to have easy access to the necessary information on the part of the investor and to create an individualized base of questions and strategies.

Finally, a lifelong learning system will have to be constructed with a lot of action and discipline. The investors can improve their knowledge and flexibility in the bond market by establishing achievable targets, making use of digital and community resources, keeping up with the changes in the industry, and being able to analyze new information critically. Such unending determination to learn not only helps investors make superior investment choices but also helps them navigate through the bond investing maze, standing tall and strong.

Chapter 11: Market Watch and Adapting Strategies

Monitoring Macroeconomic Changes

In bond investment, macroeconomic changes are important to both comprehend and observe to find one's way around the sophisticated financial markets. Investors need to maintain more vigilance in monitoring other important economic indicators, policy changes, and regulatory changes that may exert effective influence on bond markets. It is a dynamic environment that needs an advanced awareness, and one that can analyze the data, periodic releases, and economic indicators.

One of the key considerations of macroeconomic change is the need to keep in touch with what central banks are doing, most notably the Federal Reserve. The monetary policy pronouncements and actions of the Federal Reserve may have remarkable effects on the interest rates and, thus, on the bond yields. Investors should have the skill of reading such messages in order to make appropriate changes to their fixed-income strategies. To give an example, news of a future rate increase could lead to portfolio duration changes, in the sense of shifting from long to short in an effort to avoid the rise in rates, causing losses on the portfolio.

Regulatory changes are equally important in determining the bond market sphere, in addition to the policies issued by the central banks. A change would influence market accessibility and the operations of bond funds in liquidity rules or reporting standards. As an investor, it is advisable to be proactive in monitoring all these changes to ensure they are done and to align their strategies to meet the new requirements.

Product innovations also produce an effect on the bond market, that is, the introduction of smart beta or factor ETFs, ESG funds, and digital bond platforms. Investors who intend to invest in these new products should scrutinize them effectively to facilitate the addition to their portfolio. It entails the evaluation of such parameters as authenticity, liquidity, and investment objective fit. An ESG bond ETF that some ETF providers are newly launching should be vetted to make sure it only satisfies real environmental, social, and governance standards and has sufficient depth.

A statistical review of the portfolio on a periodic basis is most useful in adapting to changes in macroeconomics. Routine assessment of the portfolio, quarterly or event-driven, contributes to investors keeping on track in terms of their financial preferences. These reviews must also provide checklists of sector allocation, positioning of the yield curve, and balance across the portfolio.

Computerized digital software and accessibility to peer groups can also help investors keep up with macro developments. The availability of various tools to both research and screen where one may find reliable digital material with the use of FINRA Bond Center or Morningstar Bond Screener is an excellent insight and analysis. Further, some of the forums or social investment sites such as Bogleheads.org may provide an immediate response and the wisdom of the crowds of other investors.

It is also important to be up to date with the new strategies, products, and regulations as a bond investor. A competitive advantage can be kept through the use of educational materials (e.g., podcasts, newsletters, and webinars). Critical review and assessment of the information available, establishment of learning objectives, and development of a lifelong learning structure are some elements that enable investors to conduct a successful learning process that will enable one to navigate through any given scenario in the bond market without fear.

Finally, it is a complex process of tracking macroeconomic changes that involves being attentive, flexible, and engaging in an education process. With these skills, the bond investors will be able to preserve a lot of their wealth and maximize their income-earning skills, even in the vagaries of the financial markets.

Adjusting Portfolios for Market Shifts

Finding trends in contact investing and the skill of adapting portfolios to the swings of the market are essential qualities for pursuing the purpose of safeguarding and expanding the money possessed. The process starts with a keen body of macroeconomic indicators and regulatory shifts, as these usually initiate the requirement of portfolio editing. Bond investors should constantly be aware of things like interest rate fluctuations, inflation levels, and any fluctuation in fiscal policies, since any of these can significantly affect both bond valuation and yield.

Rebalancing is one of the most important portfolio management strategies that must be used during market transitions because risk tolerance and financial objectives of an investor remain in line. Rebalancing may be implemented when certain dates on the calendar appear or trigger rebalancing when some particular limits on deviation from target allocation have been reached. This systematic manner allows for reducing risks that could arise due to wild fluctuations in the market by maintaining a level of exposure among various kinds of sectors and by credit quality.

Moreover, the strategy of sector rotation is a sectoral strategy that investors can use to take advantage of changing economic conditions. Through sector rotation, investors are able to identify an area of the market that is likely to grow in the future, as well as minimize the risk of investing in an area of the market that is likely to experience stagnation due to the presence of headwinds. This involves a lot of insight into the economic cycle and also the ability to predict which sectors are likely to perform better under the existing climate.

Another essential element of adapting the portfolios to the market changes is the position of the yield curve. The yield curve is a plot of the yields of bonds with different maturities, and is used to indicate expectations on interest rates. Investors can make the decisions to have portfolio modifications, that is, long to short portfolios as a result of an expected rise in interest rates soon, or the other way around. This is a strategic change that can be utilized to control interest rate risk and maximize return.

Other than these classic ways of investment, the investors should also be willing to seek new product innovation in the bond industry. The new opportunities in diversification and risk reduction are with the appearance of smart beta and factor ETFs, ESG funds, and digital bond platforms. Yet, critical analysis of these products, in terms of authenticity, liquidity, and suitability in line with investment goals, is needed prior to their portfolio inclusion.

An active and continuing portfolio review is part and parcel of a stable investment approach. Investors are advised to have regular review times, which can be done on a quarterly basis or in the wake of some major market actions. This practice will keep the portfolio healthy so that it can manage the uncertainties in the market and take advantage of them.

The rebalancing of portfolios with regard to market changes is not a single process that would have to be completed once; rather, it is a continuous process that demands attention, flexibility, and dedication to natural decision-making. The systematic process of monitoring economic indicators, rebalancing portfolios, rotating sectors, and positioning on the yield curve allows investors to effectively control risks and optimise their returns in the ever-evolving business environment.

Evaluating Product Innovations

In the dynamic environment that this field represents, it is important for investors, either novice or experienced, to keep up-to-date on the latest products available in the bond market. The bond market is dynamic, and new products are appearing in the market to satisfy the varying investor needs as well as changes in the economic environment and neutral developments in technology. Learning about these innovations and critically approaching them can have an important effect on the investment strategies and benefits.

The other prominent trend of the past few years is the increase in so-called smart beta and factor-centered Exchange-Traded Funds (ETFs). The products provide exposure to certain factors, including value, growth, and volatility, to generate possible higher returns or mitigate risks relative to the market-cap weighted indices. An analysis of these products would involve knowledge of the factors that they are seeking to address and a review of their construction methodology to ascertain that they can be in line with investment objectives and the risk tolerance.

The other major field of innovation is the rise of Environmental, Social, and Governance (ESG) funds. The objective of raising these funds is to offer a return against the sustainability and ethical conduct of business processes. Investors who are considering ESG bond funds should pay attention to their validity by investigating the requirements the fund has set on how to classify as ESG compliant, the manner in which the fund is engaging with companies, and the disclosure of company information. Investors' ease of entering or exiting positions is also a very important consideration because liquidity can affect investments.

Bond markets have also become very easy to access and transparent due to the digital platforms. These platforms enable traders to sell and buy bonds efficiently, and this is usually done at a reduced cost and with higher efficiency compared to traditional methods. When assessing a digital bond platform, investors can ask the following questions: what kind of products do they provide, how convenient working on the provided platform is, and what service and support can be offered.

Investors need to take a proactive approach in assessing new product developments. This will include frequent evaluation of the portfolio holdings, being up to date on the new products and legislative changes, and seeing how these innovations can be incorporated into their investment strategy. Periodical, i.e., the so-called portfolio check-ups, are suggested to ascertain that the portfolio is in line with what the investor wants and can take. The check-ups could be event-based, i.e., done when there is a major development in the market or on a quarterly basis.

It is also possible to improve the assessment with the use of digital tools. Bond analysis websites, apps, and calculators are great ways of giving investors ideas on the performance and appropriateness of products. The pubic forums and social investing networks hold the potential to provide peer opinions and crowd intelligence, which can at times be very valuable in determining the trends and the mood of investors.

Finally, one must remain updated on new strategies, new products, and new regulations in case bond investing is to be established. This may be done through educational means such as podcasts, webinars, and newsletters to update investors about what is happening with the market and the need to change their strategies accordingly. Developing a lifelong learning system entailing goal setting of the learning, monitoring of the learning process, and testing the new information to have credibility may also enable investors to learn how to move through the complexities of the bond market.

This could be possible by putting in a critical evaluation of the product innovations and incorporating them into investment plans relevantly, thereby ensuring that investors have more options on how to get more out of it to meet their financial objectives and have it aligned with their portfolio. Such a proactive strategy not only aids in seizing the potential opportunities but also helps to combat the potential risks of new and developing financial products.

Proactive Portfolio Review

Bond investing demands a proactive approach in keeping a review of the portfolio in a dynamic market where the complexity of the market is so intense. This strategy not only implies periodic evaluations but also the willingness to respond to unpredictable changes in the economy and changes in regulations. Investors can improve the likelihood of keeping their strategies in line with the changing market conditions by developing a quarterly or event-related practice of a portfolio check-up.

The underlying concept of a proactive portfolio review is the fact that it gives a systematic way of reviewing existing positions in terms of preset goals. This undertakes an in-depth examination of macroeconomic signals that may affect the unfolding of bond markets, which include interest rate patterns, expectations on inflation, and fiscal strategies. Investors have to remain sensitive to market-moving data releases and changes in policy, which can indicate a need to make adjustments in portfolio strategy.

As an example, one may analyze the statements of central banks such as the Federal Reserve, which will give information on how they intend to move interest rates, and consequently, impact yields and prices of the bonds. Likewise, investors can keep abreast of current regulatory changes, such as the changing liquidity stipulations on bond funds, to enable them to predict and counteract the impact of market interruptions.

Portfolio adjustments to recognize changes in the market are also pivotal in making any changes by being proactive. It could include rebalancing, sector rotation, and yield curve trading. Another example is where an investor anticipates a signal of a rate hike and opts to change from a long to short duration to ensure he/she has disposed of interest rate risk. These types of strategic adjustments would involve a proper appreciation of the prevailing economic situation and its capacity to predict any consequences on bond prices.

The bond arena also requires innovation, and in doing this, it requires a proactive stance. As more smart beta/factor ETFs, ESG funds, and digital bond platforms are launched, investors need to be very critically judgmental about the genuineness and liquidity of new products. This screening operation comprises knowing the methodologies underpinning these kinds of products and how appropriate they are in an increased investment strategy.

To enable a portfolio revision process to be ongoing, digital technologies and peer groups are resources that can be incredibly valuable. Online platforms enable people to access real-time information, studies, and analysis, helping the investor to make wise decisions. It can also involve peer communities, forums, and social investing platforms that could give insights and real-time feedback, allowing one to increase proactive responses to the market value.

Moreover, it is essential to keep abreast of recent strategies, products, and regulations that can help you gain a competitive advantage in bond investing. To stay updated on the recent trends and innovations, it is possible to subscribe to the major podcasts, newsletters, and webinars on fixed income. The development of a lifelong learning system with definite objectives and a system of monitoring progress guarantees the continuous improvement and flexibility to adjust investment strategies.

The final aim of a proactive portfolio review is to enable investors to secure their wealth and get income in the form of bonds, independent of the market fluctuations. With a structured process of tracking and readjusting portfolios, investors will feel secure within the complications of bond markets. They will have a chance to grab opportunities that may come their way.

Chapter 12: Execution and Order Placement

Placing Orders Online

In an age of disruption in bond investing, it is discernible through the digital revolution that has profoundly redrawn the lines of bond investing among investors. Online sites have become crucial, and the process of buying and selling bonds has become easy, especially for newer investors and experienced ones. These sites simplify the technicalities of bond trading and create a user-friendly platform that gives investors a lot of ease when navigating the platforms.

The initial process of trading in online bonds will be to open an account with a brokerage. Such websites as Fidelity, Schwab, or Vanguard contain full access to bond markets and give investors access to a large assortment of choices: government bonds and corporate bonds. Registration is usually done on the mere requirements of personal information, some financial expense, and sometimes, a minimum deposit. When the account has been set up, investors get access to numerous tools that will assist them in making informed decisions.

Among the most valuable characteristics of online bond trading platforms is the possibility of looking at the bonds with specific requirements. Players are able to sort out options using maturity dates, credit rating, etc., and yields should be expected. This careful sifting out allows the investor to choose in line with his/her financial objectives, whether aimed at realising short-term liquidity needs or long-term stability of income.

Other essential elements of online bond trading are order types. There are numerous order types that an investor can select, such as market orders, limit orders, or all-or-none orders. Market orders can either sell or buy a bond at the current market rate, whereas limit orders provide investors with a price limit at which they are ready to sell or buy. The all-or-none order guarantees that the order will be filled all at once, which is good to have in thinly traded markets where all will not fill the order, hence inefficient allocation of portfolio adjustment.

Our platforms go beyond the fundamentals of doing simple orders; they tend to be more advanced in terms of analysis and strategy development. Being simple in its interface, investors can also have access to yield calculators, risk assessment tools, and research links that can help them single out the opportunities and risks of their trades. Moreover, most of these platforms also offer learning materials, including webinars and tutorials, which can assist the investor in developing a better knowledge about bond markets as well as improving his or her investment strategy.

Although online platforms can be described as very useful, there are some challenges and peculiarities associated with them. Another essential aspect that the investor should note is that the platform-specific terms and processes may differ widely across the providers. The variations in terms of how accrued interest is shown or how dates of settlement are confirmed may cause problems that are not well managed, with the result being confusion and errors.

To avoid the possible obstacle, investors are advised to have an adequate amount of time to get used to the platform and understand how it works and what features it offers. Most platforms provide their users with a walk-through or demo accounts that simulate real trading environments, and users thus get a chance to feel comfortable in a no-risk real trading environment.

In brief, online purchases of bonds have decimated the playing field in the bond markets, such that individuals can easily indulge in a move that was only enjoyed by institutional buyers. With the help of such tools and resources present on such digital platforms, investors will be able to perform their trading activities more precisely and thus have greater confidence in terms of reaching their financial goal.

Avoiding Execution Mistakes

When it comes to bond investing, effective implementation of trades is just as important as decision-making behind those trades. Implementation mishaps can devour returns and create excesses, thereby necessitating investors to be sharp and knowledgeable. This segment examines the traps to avoid when trading in bonds and offers knowledge on how to avoid these traps, which can cost a lot.

Paying too much to acquire a security is one of the most common mistakes related to the aspect of bond trading, because of accepting a large bid-ask spread in a shallow market. Spreads can be broader in thinly traded markets, and this fact can make a bond much more costly. Investors must be careful and think about placing limit orders to regulate the price of purchase, not buying at costs that are higher than they should be. Limit orders enable the investor to state a maximum price no more than they want to pay, where they will have some buffer against the nature of the fluctuating market and over-compensation.

One more common mistake is buying bonds that have little or no trading activity, and this is what is commonly called buying a dead CUSIP. Non-traded bonds in the hands of investors may be a source of liquidity risks as it becomes difficult to sell them without any loss. Before a trade is executed, one must make sure that there is enough trading activity and liquidity. By using sites that can show the full history of trades, the investor can determine the degree of trading activity on a bond, thereby evaluating it as an investment tool.

Investors also have to be careful of making certain mistakes that are exclusive to certain types of bonds and trading conditions. As an example, an initial tax status of a municipal bond may be determined incorrectly, which will result in unforeseen tax demands. Municipal bonds usually provide tax-free interest to the federal government and, in some cases, state and local taxes, depending on the issuer and the geographical position of the investor. Before purchasing a bond, it is imperative to know the impact of paying taxes to avoid a minor tax surprise.

Moreover, investors may end up exposing themselves to exchange rate risks by purchasing foreign bonds without taking into account the currency settlement. Investors are advised to pay attention to the currency that a foreign bond is priced in and how exchange rate movements could affect the returns when buying International bonds. The use of hedging techniques or selection of bonds within stable currencies can alleviate some of these risks.

To avoid all these execution errors, investors should use a systematic trading strategy in bonds. This would involve the prudent application of checklists to ensure the critical details of price, yield, liquidity, and settlement terms are secured prior to settling on any trade. Through a structured procedure, investors are in a better position to minimize the chances of any mistakes and enhance the overall effectiveness of bond investment procedures.

Finally, any investor should learn the lessons of other people. The constant learning and keeping abreast of the new trading methods and technologies can assist investors in optimizing their approach to execution. With patience and due diligence, investors can engage in the practice of bond trading with relative ease, as they do not fall into the pitfalls of such investments but are able to realize the best outcome of their investment.

Understanding Order Types

When it comes to bond investing, it can be of crucial importance to use the right order type in order to trade profitably. The various types of orders each have a distinct purpose, and they can greatly affect the result of a transaction. Such types should be known by investors to maneuver through the bond market effectively and to match the trading strategy with their investment goals.

Market order is one of the most popular types of orders. This form of order is adopted when an investor seeks to buy or sell a bond at the best available price at the moment. Market orders are simple to use, and there is no doubt that they would be executed, but not at the price at which the trade would run. Specifically, this may be vital in a fluctuating market in which prices may sharply fluctuate, leading to an unfavorable execution price as compared to some calculation.

Unlike limit orders, limit orders allow one to exercise some control over the acquisition price. Under a limit order, the investor provides the highest amount he/she is willing to pay or the lowest amount they are willing to accept for a bond. This kind of order will only make the trade to be executed at that particular price or lower. Limit orders can be positive when the price volatility is high, as they can be used to prevent disadvantageous trades by an investor. However, the order is at risk of not being fulfilled since the market does not reach the stipulated price.

Another significant type of order is the AON order. With this type of order, the whole order has to be filled, or none of it will be executed. This comes in handy, especially in the bond market where the large lots of bonds can partly fill them because they are of different sizes. The AON order will be critical in such cases that the investors can either receive the amount they want completely or fail to enter into the transaction at all, especially for large or illiquid bond figures.

Stop orders, or stop-loss orders, are another technique to deal with risk in bond investing. The stop order then transforms into a market order when the bond attains the stop price. Such an order is normally employed to cap any losses or secure the income on a bond position. By putting in a stop price, an investor is able to automate selling and will minimize the emotional effect of making the trading choice or decision, and what this does is provide a disciplined technique of risk control.

Besides the ones listed, stop-limit orders have a sort of combination of stop orders and limit orders. The order is then a limit order as opposed to a market order once the stop price is met. This enables investors to enter the price at which they wish the transaction to be executed, thus giving a little more control over the trade when the stop price is triggered. However, as in the case of a limit order trading, there is the risk of the trade being unsuccessful, provided that the business cannot reach the limit price.

When trading in bonds, one must understand these types of orders and what they entail. Through the selection of the right type of order, the investor will be in a better position to control their trades, execute their prices, and be able to get rid of risk. Both types of orders have their own merits and demerits, and the preferences of each one will be defined by the strategy of the investor, the condition of the market, and the particular purpose of using it. Being well-versed in these instruments can give investors an edge in making good bond-related decisions, streamlining their trading activities in the bond market, both in regard to their current trading environment and future long-term commitment.

Using Checklists for Success

In the field of bond investments, it is necessary to discuss the importance of checklists in their careful application, which may be the key to their success. These organised Blueprints act as a map and they help the investors manoeuvre the complex bond markets in a most precise and forethought manner. A checklist is about simplifying a complex process into digestible tasks and making sure that no important aspects are ignored when aiming at lucrative investments.

A checklist is a strategic tool, and hence, it is important to start with the basic stage of defining the investment objectives. Effective goal setting helps an investor define their strategy to fit their particular financial targets; whether it is income generation, capital preservation, or diversification, goals are clearly defined to allow the investor to set their tactical programs accordingly. This sense of purpose serves as a guide, one that indicates the following actions in the investing process.

The following is the emphasis on the thorough assessment of the possible investment in bonds. This refers to a detailed study of the nature of the bond, such as credit rating, yield, maturity, and embedded options. The checklists remind one to question the presence of these factors so that every bond being considered should be within the overall portfolio strategy and the risk appetite of the investor.

The Bond market environment is dynamic, and whenever there is a variation in macroeconomic factors and regulatory changes, it is important to be aware of them. Checklists will help investors remember the need to review interest rate trends, inflation expectations, and policy changes that potentially influence bond valuations on a regular basis. With adequate management, these external forces can be dealt with methodically, allowing the investors to make informed decisions that will boost the resilience and performance of their portfolio.

Another ultra-important step is implementation, and therein lies the value of checklists. They give instructions on how to trade and a guide to follow the process of the trade, starting with verifying the trade information and developments through the end of the regulation compliance of the trade. Such a form of organization reduces errors and ensures a smooth process of transaction, hence protecting the interests of the investor.

Moreover, checklists include the necessity of continual work on portfolio management. They also advise that the holding in the bond should be reviewed periodically to evaluate performance and make the necessary moves when circumstances demand them due to the fluctuating nature of the market. This active action assists in keeping the portfolio in line with the goals of the investor, and the portfolio would therefore be in a position to support the financial goals of the investor in the long run.

Finally, careful application of checklists can allow the investor to enter the bond investing jungle without fear. Checklists result in the improvement of the decision-making process because they help in breaking down the investment process into several steps that can be acted upon. Hence, the chances of having an oversight are very low. They make what would otherwise be an overwhelming task into a systematic, manageable, and ultimately successful task. So, checklists are not just a tool at all, but they are a strategy, and they create a culture of conscientiousness and accuracy, which are very necessary ingredients to succeed in the world of bond investing.

Chapter 13: Real-World Case Studies

Market Turmoil and Bond Portfolios

When markets become wild and unpredictable, bond portfolios tend to be a source of stability in what is otherwise financial market turbulence. The volatility that the equity markets see can be well addressed through good bond portfolios that would maintain the wealth of an investor and provide a steady flow of income. The fixed amount of returns and predictable maturity dates make bonds a more secure option than equities, making them the preferred option amongst risk-averse investors.

Bonds have proved to be stabilizing in the course of a market downturn, as witnessed during the 2008 and 2020 financial crises. Unlike stocks, which are subject to huge price variations, bonds guarantee a known rate of return that is predetermined when the bond is purchased. It puts them in a better position to avoid the uncertainties of market sentiment and cushions against volatility, which tends to follow in the wake of economic turmoil.

The position of bonds as part of an investment portfolio cannot be underrated. They serve to diversify individual efforts and as a safeguard to the more risky equity investments. The price of the bond may increase when the stock prices are down and panic is developing in the market (i.e., during the times of market stress). This is one of the main ideas of portfolio diversification, as the inclusion of bonds is essential to such a strategy since most stocks and bonds are supposed to move inversely with each other.

There are not very few hiccups with bond portfolios, at least not in a low-interest-rate environment. There is an intricate environment of interest rate, credit, and reinvestment risks, which investors need to overcome. The risk of interest rates is also applicable, and an increasing interest rate can cause a decrease in the price of the bond. These risks of being exposed to vagaries of the market can be controlled by selecting bonds with different maturities and qualities to reach a balance in investments.

Also, bond portfolio allocation can be made according to the planned investment goals. Investors who need income to support their lifestyle can also find high-yield bonds to have good returns, although with risk. On the other hand, government bonds or high-grade corporate bonds will better suit individuals who pay great importance to safety. The trick here is to match the bond portfolio with the risk appetite of the investor, horizon, and financial aspirations.

In the event of volatility in the market, the flexibility provided by the bond portfolio becomes the most prioritized factor. Investors need to be ready to modify their portfolios, which consist of bonds, due to changes in economic times. This can be a movement towards short-term as compared to long-term bonds when interest rates are projected to go up and vice versa, as well as a rising exposure to inflation-linked securities during inflationary times.

Finally, the value of bond portfolios is that they are able to give stability and income, even in times when the markets are jittery. The key to protecting your financial future is being able to see the dynamics in relation to bonds, as well as using proper risk management techniques. It is highly likely that as the financial environment continues to change, the place of bonds as a pillar of a sound financial investment plan will not change in any way.

Case Studies in Bond Mispricing

In the complex environment of bond investing, mispricing is a potential serious issue and a profitable opportunity for investors. Mispricing is a condition in which the price at which the participants trade a bond in a market does not reflect the actual value of the bond based on its intrinsic properties. The result of these discrepancies may be used by the investors who can detect and implement them to achieve the maximum returns.

Consider a typical situation of bond mispricing, i.e., this can be traced in thinly traded markets; wide bid-ask spreads in thinly traded markets are due to the absence of frequent transactions. When such environments occur, investors may end up paying more on bonds by agreeing with such wide spreads since they have no clear understanding of the conditions in the market, or they are unable to enter into negotiations. It is especially common in the corporate bond market, where liquidity may be very scarce and where pricing transparency may be minimal. One should be careful as an investor and do their due diligence to avoid paying excessively in such cases.

The other situation is buying bonds where there may be no or minimal trade activity, commonly known as buying into a dead CUSIP. They may have been issued many years ago. Because there is no interest in the market over a long period, their market prices may not be taken into consideration in the current market, and the creditworthiness of the issuer. Investors acquiring these bonds without much research are likely to have a hard time selling or ending up with bonds that may lose value because of unexpected credit events.

The municipal bond market is one more area where mispricing may occur due to the important role of tax factors in the valuation. A typical error that is made is the failure to interpret the tax status of the purchase of a municipal bond. Investors may purchase a bond and think that it is tax-free, when in reality, it is not, or they may not think about the consequences of the Alternative Minimum Tax (AMT) on an investment return. These oversights can result in self-appointed taxation, and thus, the net interest on the bond is decreased, which affects the overall returns of the investor.

In the international bond market, there may be mispricing due to the issue of currency settlement. Investors who buy foreign bonds without the effects of currency risks may find themselves in a situation where they experience a lot of volatility in their returns because of the exchange rates. This may cause situations when the face yield looks very tempting; however, the underlying value, when taking into account the effect of the currency fluctuations, is quite a bit lower.

Investors must prepare a well-laid-out list before going into such mispricing situations. This involves verifying the price of the bond, yield, liquidity, and settlement details of any bond before making any deal. Investors must learn to be patient and do due diligence by conducting ongoing education on their part in an attempt to improve their knowledge of the operations of the bond market. Only by finding out what went wrong, their mistakes should be considered as the sources of information that help investors in avoiding a repetition of such mistakes in the future and better position themselves to reap the consequences of mispricing opportunities, with results of a considerably reduced risk. This kind of strategic foresight is necessary in the process of ensuring that a bond portfolio is successful despite the market inefficiencies.

Successful Bond Investing Strategies

When it comes to investing in bonds, success lies in learning and applying successful tactics that will ensure not only the base short-term financial objectives but also create stability in the invested portfolio to withstand turbulence. An effective bond investment plan is a combination of skills, formalities, and flexibility to deal with fluctuations in the market. Diversification is one of the core plans that is used as a tool in the minimization of risk. A range of bond investments (i.e., a mix of government, municipal, and corporate bonds) would allow an investor to diversify his/her portfolio, to mitigate the effects of volatility that can be attached to one type of bond. The same can be diversified towards bonds with different maturity and credit ratings, hence increasing the security of returns.

One of the most important techniques that the most profitable bond investors have used is the development of a bond ladder. In this strategy, one will mainly acquire the bonds whose maturities would be staggered, whereby the bond matures, it replaces the principal by acquiring new bonds. Not only does this bring a hassle-free regular inflow, but it also reduces the risk of losing due to interest rate changes. Investors have the opportunity to diversify reinvestment risks with a laddered portfolio and take advantage of an increase in rates without having to speculate about how the market will move in the future.

Another tactical combination is the barbell or bullet portfolios, the framework that seeks to exploit certain interest rate regimes. A barbell strategy is investing in short-term and long-term bonds, whereas a bullet strategy is investing in long-term bonds that are going to mature at a similar time. These tactics will come in handy in unorganized interest-rate environments and enable investors to attain the right balance between risk and returns of their bond holdings.

Also, it is essential to be highly mindful of interest rate trends. The implications of duration and convexity can be better understood and can help investors enormously manage interest rate risk. The duration of a bond is an indicator of how sensitive this bond is to fluctuations in interest rates. In contrast, convexity is an indicator of the curvature in the relationship between price and the yield of a bond. Through these measurements, investors are able to calibrate their portfolio on expected interest rate fluctuations, thus maximizing their investment.

Best-performing investors in the bonds also use hedging to cushion themselves against adverse changes in the markets. This may include such derivatives brought in to hedge against the interest rate risks, like the Treasury futures and swaps. When well implemented, these strategies enable the investors to control any losses they may be facing without compromising the possibility of realizing gains.

Another feature of a successful strategy is to incorporate the use of scenario analysis into the investment process. This is done by running simulations of different conditions in the market and how such market activity will affect the bond portfolio. Through all these, investors are able to plan and even modify the strategy towards any eventual possibility. This proactive style is what keeps portfolios updated with the condition of the market and individual investment objectives.

Lastly, one must have a disciplined rebalancing strategy. Ensuring that a bond portfolio has the desired risk profile by reviewing and making the necessary adjustments on a regular basis assists in ensuring that the asset allocation of the portfolio remains. This practice not only allows a portfolio to lock in gains but is also useful in reducing the losses in a portfolio so that they can be set back on track to achieve long-term financial goals.

To sum it all up, effective bond investing demands the consideration of a variety of strategies depending on individual needs and market circumstances. Incorporating diversification, rational portfolio construction, interest rate sensitivity, hedging, scenario analysis, and active rebalancing, therefore, enables investors to master the intricacies of bond markets and to do so with a confidence that can generate sustainable, long-term success.

Learning from Mistakes

One of the most common mistakes in investing in stocks is similar to any other investment case, such as bonds. This is not to say that the mistakes are merely hiccups; they represent a rare and invaluable learning experience that can make the investor crafty and a better decision-maker. It is important to pay attention to and suss out these errors so that when entering the bond investment world, it will be a lot easier to navigate through.

The major category of pitfalls in the bond investment is paying too much for a bond by taking on a poorly formed spread in a thin market. It is counterproductive, since the investor has to pay more than he or she should to acquire the bond in the first place; hence, the expected returns become relatively insignificant, and the risk of losing money becomes high. That usually occurs when the market liquidity is low, and there are no fair prices to be found. Investors can curtail this brain fart by doing good market research and setting limit orders to dictate the price of purchase.

The other common pitfall is purchasing a dead CUSIP, which is a bond that has no or very little volume. These bonds are not easily sold, and this brings liquidity problems. By confirming the trading volume of the bond and making sure that there is enough interest in an investment, investors can avoid this.

Mistakes also tend to be made when it comes to the tax status of municipal bonds. It is prudent that one understands the tax implications of purchasing a municipal bond to avoid any surprises in the future in the form of unexpected tax bills. Investors ought to pay attention to the tax position of a bond, bearing in mind that they may be exempt from barriers of federal, state, and local taxes. Such knowledge can have a considerable influence on the carried net yield of this investment, and it is one of the main factors in the decision-making process.

Cross-border bonds have yet another set of obstacles, especially when it comes to the consideration of settlement in currency. When an investor purchases a foreign bond, he/she does not take into consideration the currency risk of such an investment, and this may cause great losses in case of unfortunate changes in the exchange rates. Investors are also advised to protect themselves against currency risk or invest in home currency bonds in order to reduce such risk.

To arm these investors with things they shall use to avoid these pitfalls, solutions and checklists shall be given to them. Every scenario must be followed by certain steps that investors can go through to ensure they make the right decision before making any trade. This may involve verifying the type of a bond in terms of its price, yield, liquidity, and settlement conditions.

In addition, the best way to learn is by observing others make errors. It reiterates the fact that you should be patient, diligent in your work, and continue educating yourself. With such an approach, the investor would be able to analyze past mistakes and thus work out a more careful and knowledgeable method, which, in the long run, would bring more profitability to bond investing.

Investing in bonds permits making mistakes entirely, as rather than being an unwelcome event, it is an educational experience. All the mistakes are also accompanied by a lesson that, upon learning, one can have better investment control and performance. By acknowledging and observing these errors, investors will be able to develop and perfect their methodologies and provide better ideas about the bond market, which will lead to more prosperous investment decisions.

Chapter 14: Conclusion and Next Steps

Recap of Key Concepts

When it comes to the bond investment field of knowledge, the most important step is to gain an axiomatic knowledge of the subject and then apply it within the financial realm. Bonds, in essence, are the loan an investor gives to the issuer, which is either an individual firm, a government, or any other issuer. In exchange, the investor gets periodic interest on his money and the return of the money at the end of the period. This background knowledge preconditions the further development of the jungle of bond markets.

One of the essential features of bonds is that they are used in portfolio diversification. The difference between bonds and stocks is that bonds can be viewed as a stabilizing influence, as they have a stabilizing effect on the stock market. Bonds may serve as safe havens during turbulent times in the markets, protecting capital and allowing reliable income in terms of interest payments. This feature makes them an effective part of a diversified portfolio, especially for those risk-averse investors who are willing to obtain regular returns.

Interest rates play a critical role in bond investment and affect bond prices and yields. An increase in the interest rate normally leads to a decline in the price of existing bonds and vice versa. This negative connection is one that investors should understand very well because it affects the pricing of the bonds and the returns that you can earn. One must understand the yield to maturity (YTM), which computes the total amount of returns one is likely to earn if one holds onto a bond until completion of its term.

The other important concept is diversification to the bond sector itself. Bonds differ in terms of the form of the bond and characteristics, as well as the risk level associated with each. The Government bonds, including the U.S. Treasuries, are normally low risk since the government backs them. The yields of corporate bonds are, however, higher as they compensate for higher risk. In the interim, municipal bonds are preferable to others because of their tax benefits to a specific category of investors. Being aware of these differences enables investors to customize their portfolio based on their risk and return requirements.

The duration concept also plays a crucial role as it becomes a measure of the sensitivity of bonds against changes in interest rates. The longer the duration of a bond, the more it is susceptible to rise and fall in interest rates compared to shorter ones. This measure assists investors in the process of deciding between their bond choice and their interest rate basis and risk concern.

Another critical concept is the credit risk, which is said to represent the risk of default by an issuer to honour obligations. Credit ratings are information given by such agencies as Moody's and Standard & Poor's to establish the financial capability of an issuer and his or her state of default. Investors have to balance these ratings with profits to make better decisions.

In addition, different types of bond structures should be known, including callable, putable, and convertible bonds. These characteristics influence both the yield and risk of a bond and so represent future chances of making astute investment choices according to market variables.

To conclude, a sound understanding of the following concepts- the interest rates, the diversification, the duration, the credit risks, and the bond structures is the backbone of effective bond investment. The principles will not only enable the investors to mitigate the risks, but also go a notch higher and enable them to take advantage of market opportunities, thus creating a balanced and robust investment portfolio.

Empowering the Bond Investor

When some bonds are considered in bond investing, one must understand how the market works so as to make better decisions concerning one's money and one's desired expectations. With all these options and problems located within this complex environment, it is no wonder that investors are looking to make their way and find solutions that are relevant to them. Nevertheless, they can achieve a new level and become stable with the help of proper knowledge and tools, and turn these issues into opportunities.

One of the key factors in empowering bond investors is to provide them with the skill of evaluating and reading signs in the market. This relates to how interest rates, inflation, and economic indicators move the bond prices and yields. By understanding these theories, investors can make intelligent portfolio decisions that can maximize the way the portfolio option will be emphasized under current and future market environments.

Besides, investors should be well equipped to scrutinize the credit rating of the bond issuers. This necessitates an in-depth knowledge of credit ratings, financial statements, and sector-specific risks. Individuals are able to analyze the credits diligently so that they can detect any risk and benefit before decisively making decisions on bonds that they want in their portfolios. This requires a lot of analysis and is vital in the elimination of default risks and in having a consistent stream of cash flow in the form of interest earnings.

The next critical factor in empowering the bond sector investors is that there is an opportunity to create distributed portfolios that take into account risks and their returns. This means that diversification into a mixture of bonds with different maturities, credit ratings, and sectors comprises the repertoire of bonds to curb risks that arise due to market fluctuations. Diversification also helps by guarding against any specific defaulting of a bond and maximizing each sector of the bond market, depending on the economy that is doing well at that given moment.

To further improve the quality of your bond investing, you also need to get into how more advanced financial instruments can work in your favor. Such instruments as callable and putable bonds, convertible bonds, and inflation-protected securities offer the advantage of customizing portfolios to personal financial objectives and market preferences. These tools provide versatility with regard to interest rate risk control, acquisition of capital appreciation, and safeguarding against inflationary forces.

Additionally, to make the bond investment more constructive, the application of innovative technologies and digitalization can be of great help. Financial calculators and online platforms allow investors to dissect bond characteristics, monitor performance, and make trading faster and more accurate. These tools deliver real-time data and insights and help investors make their decisions promptly to achieve the best results in their investments.

Lastly, to ensure a competitive advantage, bond investors must remain updated with respect to any regulatory change or any innovation within the marketplace. These are factors like being able to comprehend tax implications, compliance requirements, and solutions such as ESG (Environmental, Social, and Governance) investing. As they track such trends, investors will be able to realign their strategies with the changing market forces and regulatory environments.

To conclude, the empowerment of investors in bonds is a complex process that requires a combination of educational, strategic, and advanced means of analysis and the implementation of technologies. With the knowledge of these aspects, the investor is in a good position to undertake the challenge of the bond market, safeguard their money, and meet their financial goals. This power not only helps one to be more financially stable but also helps to build a stronger and more agile investment portfolio.

Engaging with Community Resources

In the global world of bond investing, it is a good idea to have access to the community resources to magnify the investor experience and information. The specialty of the community resources is that we can share our discoveries, strategies, and experiences among the investors, which can be of great use to a budding investor who has to deal with the complexity of bond markets. The resources do not only relate to learning but also to practical application and up-to-date market intelligence.

Access to a repository of knowledge is one of the key advantages of utilizing community resources. Online communities. One of the general forums on investing, like Reddit: r/investing or Bogleheads.org, in general, online forums and social media related to investing are available, where an investor can ask their questions and get responses to them from other members who have probably already encountered the same issue. The use of these platforms can be vital when it comes to discussing the current market situation, looking at macroeconomic indicators, and coming up with ideas on how to adjust the portfolio to such conditions. The face-to-face, informal nature of such exchanges is real-time interaction, which is an evolving learning situation matched to the market.

Other than the forums, local investment clubs also provide one with the chance of learning and networking face-to-face. At these clubs, meetings are usually held, with guest speakers, workshops, and group discussions forming part of the events. Different topics continue to be addressed regarding bond investments, including understanding yield curves and the introduction of new financial instruments. The involvement in such clubs can result in the development of mentorships and partnerships, creating an atmosphere in which the new investors would be able to go through the experience of the experienced professionals.

Digital resources and tools are also necessary when connecting with community resources. Such websites as FINRA Bond Center or Morningstar Bond Screener provide full-scale platforms for bond research and investigation of trends within the bond market, as well as an opportunity to screen the bonds in terms of investment. Such tools are frequently accompanied by educational materials that inform the investor about relevant concepts like bond pricing, calculation of yields, etc.

Additionally, financial experts offer podcasts and webinars focused on existing trends and prospects within the sphere of the bond market, in extremely detailed explanations and discussions. It is also good to sign up for newsletters from reputable financial institutions in the country, which are very helpful in informing investors about changes in regulations, market predictions, and new products in the bond market. These materials are especially helpful in learning about new trends, such as green bonds and ESG (Environmental, Social, and Governance) investing, which are becoming more popular among investors interested in being environmentally friendly.

Moreover, the connections one gets when he/she interact with community resources avenues can be relied on as a support system to assist an investor in the event of making a difficult decision or in the face of falling markets. This network can give both emotional and strategic support, which can assist the investors in ensuring that they have a long-term focus when in an environment of volatility and that they stick to their investment plans. Social support can be provided by the experiences and common wisdom of the wider community, which can be the stabilizing factor, as support and advice are given at the critical moments.

To sum up, combining community resources with a bond investing strategy is a great approach in numerous ways, including obtaining more knowledge and skills, as well as emotional and strategic advice. Through such active involvement in such communities, investors can enhance their decision-making process, remain updated on happenings in the market, and through all this, confidently and more resiliently meet their end financial objective. Online tools, local clubs, and digital tools, in general, represent the core part of a successful bond investment experience as a means to engage with community resources.

The Path Forward in Bond Investing

With the current state of change in the bond investment environment, investors must adjust and develop the required efficiency to ensure they are able to traverse the meanderings of the contemporary financial climate. The future of bond investing lies in a more complex process that would combine old and new approaches to make portfolios more developed and flexible in terms of dynamically emerging market conditions.

An important feature of the next step is the realization of the macroeconomic trends' interaction with the bond markets. Bond investors have to be aware of global economic indicators, interest rate policy, and geopolitical events, which may determine the yields and the price of bonds. Keeping these factors in mind, an investor would be able to align his/her portfolio in a manner that would help it assume maximum profits at the expense of risk.

One thing that has been emphasized in successful bond investing is diversification. Not only does it diversify investments in different sectors and credit quality, but it also includes the usage of different types of bonds, such as government, corporate, municipal, and international bonds. All those categories have different risks and returns, and by combining them, it is possible to create more stable and better-performing portfolios. Bonds diversification can be further achieved through diversification of bonds with equities and alternative assets that further reduce the portfolio volatility and match the investment strategy with the personal financial requirements.

The other important aspect moving forward is rebalancing. Periodic portfolio examinations ensure that preferred asset allocations and risks are maintained. To make sure that their portfolios are aligned with investment goals, the investors are expected to utilize signal-based and rebalancing strategies, which are calendar-based and threshold-based. This field makes the effects of the market fluctuation minimal and, as such, keeps the portfolio in line with its long-term objectives.

Using innovative forms of bonds and techniques is also necessary for a contemporary bond investor. Knowledge and management of vehicles such as callable bonds, inflation-indexed (TIPS), and high-yield bonds can be further points of diversification and the possible increase in yield. Both risks and opportunities accompany all these instruments, and they have to be analyzed correctly and set as part of the bigger picture.

In the future, technology will be a key issue in bond investment. The emergence of digital platforms and devices provides investors with new opportunities to access information on the current condition of the market, research, and opportunities to do transactions. With the help of these tools, investors can make the right decisions and trade effectively. Also, it is advisable to follow online communities and educational resources that may increase understanding and ensure that investors are updated on the current market changes and innovations.

Last but not least, an educational and transformation process is essential. The bond market is ever evolving due to the emergence of new products, the occurrence of changes in regulations, and economic factors. Investors should embrace a culture of being lifelong learners and open themselves up to make any necessary changes in the way they do things when new information arises. This aggressiveness gives the investors the best chance to maneuver through the vagaries of the bond market and enjoy the new opportunities that come their way.

To sum up, the new orientation in bond investing can be described as the combination of classic knowledge and trying some innovative solutions in this field. With this knowledge, a good portfolio (meaning abundant and diversified), returning, rebalancing, and use of technology, as well as life-long learning, an investor will be free to weather the complex issues of the bond market and meet his/her investment goals.

EPILOGUE

As readers conclude "**Bond Investing for Beginners**," a profound understanding of the intricacies of bond markets and their crucial role in wealth preservation and income generation is within grasp. This book has meticulously dismantled complex concepts, transforming them into accessible knowledge for investors at every stage of their journey. The essence of bond investing has been laid bare, from foundational principles to advanced strategies, ensuring that readers are equipped to navigate even the most turbulent market conditions with confidence.

Throughout the chapters, the emphasis has been on empowering investors to make informed decisions. By demystifying bond jargon, illustrating the importance of risk management, and providing detailed frameworks for portfolio construction, this book serves as a comprehensive guide for those seeking financial security through fixed income investments. The strategies outlined are not just theoretical; they are actionable, designed to be directly implemented in real-world scenarios.

In a financial landscape often characterized by volatility, bonds offer a pillar of stability. The insights shared here underscore bonds' role as a tool for achieving consistent income and safeguarding wealth against market downturns. The discussions on various bond types, from municipals to corporates, and the exploration of advanced instruments like TIPS and ESG bonds, have expanded the reader's toolkit, enabling a tailored approach to investing that aligns with personal goals and market conditions.

The journey through this book also highlights the importance of ongoing education and adaptation. As markets evolve, so too must the strategies employed by astute investors. This book encourages a proactive approach, urging readers to continue exploring new developments and innovations in the bond market, ensuring their portfolios remain robust and resilient.

Ultimately, "**Bond Investing for Beginners**" aims to instill a sense of empowerment, fostering a mindset where investors are not merely reactive to market changes but are strategic in their approach to financial growth and preservation. As you close this book, carry forward the knowledge and confidence to make bond investing a cornerstone of your financial strategy, securing your wealth and generating income in any market climate.

www.ingramcontent.com/pod-product-compliance
Lightning Source LLC
Chambersburg PA
CBHW070935210326
41520CB00021B/6953